Real Tragedy
Real Triumph

True stories and images from the crash and rebirth of Marshall University football

presented by

The Herald-Dispatch
www.herald-dispatch.com

CONTENTS

REAL TRAGEDY, REAL TRIUMPH

FOREWORD

REAL TRAGEDY, REAL TRIUMPH

By James E. Casto

There are tragic dates and events burned so deeply into America's memory that they defy time and the passage of years. It's as if they've become part of our collective DNA. Their images are as vivid as if they happened just yesterday.

Few older Americans will ever forget how the peaceful quiet of a Sunday morning was shattered on December 7, 1941, when word flashed from Hawaii that the Japanese were attacking Pearl Harbor. Most of us old enough to recall November 22, 1963, remember exactly where we were and what we were doing when we heard the awful news from Dallas: President Kennedy had been shot and killed. And certainly the terrorist attacks of September 11, 2001, will forever be engraved in the hearts and minds of Americans.

For Marshall University and Huntington, November 14, 1970, is a date etched in the same somber tones. And one never to be forgotten.

The first word that stormy Saturday night was that a plane had crashed at Tri-State Airport. Then came chilling confirmation of the suspicion that the plane was a charter jet carrying 75 Marshall football players, coaches and fans. There were no survivors.

The Marshall plane crash was headline news across the country and around the world. But the national headlines soon faded and the network TV reporters quickly moved on to the next big story. In the process, the media missed the amazing saga of a campus and community that, while still mourning lost friends and family, nonetheless picked up and went on, turning tragedy into triumph. That story has been a private one, held close to our hearts.

Now all that has changed. The Marshall story is on the big screen for the whole world to see. "We Are Marshall" tells what happened in the way only a big-budget Hollywood movie can do. It's a wonderful film, one that's likely to be enjoyed for years to come.

But here, gathered in these pages, is the *real* story – the riveting details of the plane crash and the spectacular rebirth of Marshall football, as reported in the pages of The Herald-Dispatch as the events unfolded and as those touched by them have looked back over the years.

This retelling of Marshall's remarkable story is offered for those too young to remember – and for those who will never be able to forget.

James E. Casto retired in 2004 after more than 40 years as a reporter and editor with The Herald-Dispatch. He is the author of a half-dozen books on local and regional history.

THE CRASH

THE EVENTS OF NOVEMBER 1970

THE STORY OF THE
1970 MARSHALL PLANE CRASH

By Bob Withers, The Herald-Dispatch

HUNTINGTON—Well-wishers bidding goodbye to the 75 Marshall University football players, coaches and fans who took off from Kinston, N.C., after a heartbreaking 17-14 loss to East Carolina University in Greenville, couldn't have known that was the last time they would see them alive.

Flight 932, a chartered twin-engine, 95-seat Southern Airways DC-9, had a crew of five—pilot, first officers, two strewardesses and a charter coordinator—when it departed Kinston at 6:38 p.m. Saturday, Nov. 14, 1970, for an expected 52-minute fight.

The crew established contact with controllers at Tri-State Airport at 7:23 p.m., announcing that they were descending to 5,000 feet. The controller advised them of rain, fog, smoke and a ragged ceiling. At 7:34, as the plane approached Tri-State from the West, its crew reported passing the airport's outer marker and a controller cleared them to land. The crew requested a "step three" while discussing approach lighting—flyers' jargon for medium intensity.

"Roger, that's where they are, with the rabbit (sequence flasher)," the controller answered. "Advise when you want them cut."

"Very good," the crew answered.

Those were the last words anyone heard from the plane.

Witnesses at the Ashland Oil refinery across the Big Sandy River in Kentucky saw the big aircraft overhead and thought everything was normal except that it seemed low. One witness reported hearing the roar of its engines accelerate just after it disappeared over the first hill in West Virginia, and in fact the flight data recorder—found later in the wreckage—indicated that the crew initiated an effort to scrub the

Poor weather that helped cause the disaster hampered efforts by emergency personnel. The plane clipped trees on its approach to Tri-State Airport after a 45-minute flight.

With the exception of part of the fuselage and a few small pieces, little was left of the Southern jet. Still, volunteers searched for whatever could be found to help with the investigation.

landing, go around and try again.

But at about 7:36, tower personnel saw a red glow west of the airport.

The jet had struck a tree on a hill 5,543 feet west of the runway threshold. It cut a swatch 95 feet wide and 279 feet long through other trees, leaving behind several pieces of its right wing and nose.

The plane dipped to the right, almost inverted and crashed into a hollow nose-first 4,219 feet short of the runway and about 225 feet south of the middle marker. The impact scattered engines and other parts over a wide area, and the resulting ground fire melted most of the fuselage or reduced it to a powder-like substance.

All 75 people on board died. The crash would be labeled the worst air disaster in American sports history.

A temporary morgue was set up in the National Guard armory at the airport and the painstaking and painful processes of mourning and body identification began. Obituary notices ran for several days in the pages of Huntington's newspapers.

On Sunday night, Nov. 15, a memorial service was conducted at the Memorial Field House. Moments of silence, remembrances and prayers followed in stadiums, houses of worship and meeting halls across the nation a week later.

During the following week, classes at Marshall, civic meetings and luncheons and a show sponsored by the Marshall Artists Series were canceled, and government offices were closed.

Ultimately, the bodies of six victims were never identified and, after a mass funeral at the Field House, they were buried together at Spring Hill Cemetery.

"They are still a team," said Dr. Aldred P. Wallace, then pastor of Johnson Memorial United Methodist Church.

The National Transportation Safety Board dryly concluded a year and a half later that the cause of the crash was uncertain.

" ... the probable cause of this accident was the descent below Minimum Descent Altitude during a nonprecision approach under adverse operating conditions, without visual contact with the runway environment," the report said.

The board guessed that happened because of improper use of cockpit instrumentation data or an altimetry systems error.

In these pages, you'll read the reports of the story as it unfolded, and through the words of those touched by the events, as they've looked back in more recent years. The account starts with the disappointing football game that preceded the ill-fated flight.

CONTROVERSIAL CALL ENDS CHANCES FOR TIE: EAST CAROLINA NIPS HERD 17-14

By Mike Brown, Herald-Advertiser Sports Writer

(Editor's Note: Mike Brown, who covered Saturday's ill-fated Marshall-East Carolina game, was not aboard the plane that took the Thundering Herd and its traveling party to their death. He motored to Greenville, site of the game, with his wife.)

GREENVILLE, N.C.—East Carolina University place kicker Tony Gurso kicked a 24-yard field goal with 12:27 left and that proved to be the difference as the Pirates shaded Marshall University, 17-24, Saturday afternoon before a turnout of 8,711 at Ficklen Stadium, including ex-Marshall great John Zontini.

Zontini, who was recently inducted in the West Virginia Sports Writers Hall of Fame, was seeing his alma mater play for the first time since his graduation in 1935.

Marshall, which has had its share of tough breaks this season, saw another come its way with 30 seconds remaining in the contest when quarterback Ted Shoebridge was called for intentional grounding, a call which left the Thundering Herd and its small group of fans puzzled.

The controversial call all but ended Marshall's hopes for gaining at least a tie on a day in which it turned in what coach Rich Tolley felt was a sub-par performance.

Shoebridge, who didn't get into the game until the second half, had driven the Herd 63 yards in less than one minute and was knocking on the door when the call came.

On a third and 10 at the ECU 25, Shoebridge faded to pass and was collared by the Pirates Jim Gudger at the East Carolina 44. Shoebridge got off the pass but was called for grounding the ball which carried a five-yard penalty from the spot of the call.

The pass was intended for halfback Art Harris who fielded it on the bounce.

"The ball only hit about five feet from me," explained Harris who shared everyone else's puzzlement about the call.

With any hopes of a game-tying field goal by Marcelo Lajterman

now snuffed out, he threw a futile fourth-down pass deep down field and it fell incomplete, giving the Pirates the football with only 11 seconds left.

"We had a nice flight down, but we played like we were still flying," said Tolley, who expressed displeasure with the Herd's overall play.

"We had a number of opportunities to win it," he continued, "but we couldn't capitalize."

"Our offensive execution was not as good as it has been and defensively, we just gave up too many yards on the ground. It appeared to me as though East Carolina wanted it more than we did."

East Carolina, which didn't throw a single pass in the second half, ground out 302 yards rushing with 178 of it coming in the second half.

Les Strayhorn picked up 142 yards on 28 carries and Billy Wallace added 132 on 27. Joe Hood was Marshall's leading rusher as he picked up 111 yards on 23 carries.

Quarterback John Casazza added 16 yards for the Pirates, getting six of them on a touchdown run in the second period.

The performance by the East Carolina running backs overshadowed fine defensive performances by Marshall linebacker Jerry Stainback and defensive guard Larry Brown. Stainback was in on 22 tackles, nine of them unassisted, and Brown

Quarterback Bob Harris looks for a receiver as center Rich Dardinger (50) and guard Tom Howard (60) block during Marshall's 17-14 loss to East Carolina on November 14, 1970.

was in on 18, seven unassisted.

The bright spot offensively for Marshall was Shoebridge who completed 14 of 32 passes for 188 yards in his best showing of the year. He had a touchdown pass of 16 yards to Jack Repasy in the third period.

Bob Harris, who was used only as a receiver in the second half, caught four passes for 86 yards and teamed up with Shoebridge to keep the Herd in contention.

The Pirates got excellent field position in the second period when Mike Mills covered Hood's fumble, Casazza scored his first touchdown of the season when he rolled around right end with 12:04 left in the half.

Marshall forged a 7-7 halftime tie on an electrifying 81-yard interception return by Stu Cottrell, second longest in school history, with 1:19 left in the half.

East Carolina, following a 45-yard filed goal attempt by Lajterman which fell short, drove from its own 20 to the Marshall 22 where it had a first down.

Casazza, who had completed four straight passes on the drive, attempted to pass to the right sideline. MU defensive end Dave Griffith batted the ball right back into the startled Casazza's hands and he instinctively threw the ball again. Cottrell picked the ball up in the flat and zipped down the sidelines.

Hood fumbled on the ECU 48 with Chuck Zadnik falling on the football, setting up ECU's second TD. The Pirates, aided by a face-masking call on Larry Sanders, scored in seven plays with Wallace going in from the one.

After an exchange of punts, Shoebridge moved the Herd 76 yards in only seven plays, hitting Repasy for the score with six minutes left in the third period, tying it at 14-14.

The big play in the drive came when Shoebridge hit Bob Harris for 48 yards on third and 21 from the Marshall 13. Harris took the ball on the MU 45 and carried it to the Pirates 41.

Hood got it on a halfback draw, Shoebridge and Bob Harris teamed for 12 and another first down at the 19. Shoebridge then hit Repasy in the middle of the end zone with a perfectly thrown pass.

GAME SUMMARY

Marshall 0, 7, 7, 0, 14
East Carolina 0, 7, 7, 3, 17
EC - Casazza 6 run (Guzzo kick)
M - Cottrell 81 pass int. (Lajterman kick)
EC - Wallace 1 run (Guzzo kick)
M - Repasy 19 pass from Shoebridge
    (Lajterman kick)
EC - Guzzo 24 field goal
Attendance - 8,711

STATISTICS:

	MARSHALL	ECU
First down	21	20
Yards rushing	134	290
Yards passing	210	49
Passes	17-41-2	5-14-2
Return yardage	95	81
Punts	4-38-0	6-33-0
Fumbles lost	3	1
Penalties	98	42

INDIVIDUAL LEADERS
RUSHING
Marshall: Hood 23-111, A. Harris 8-30,
    B. Harris 2-5, Shoebridge 4-(-12).
East Carolina: Stryhorn 28-142, Wallace 27-
    132, Casazza 6-16.

PASSING
Marshall: Shoebridge 14-32-1 for 188 yards and
    1 touchdown, B. Harris 3-9-1 for 22 yards.
East Carolina: Casazza 5-14-2 for 49 yards.

RECEIVING
Marshall: Hood 5-55; B. Harris 4-86, A. Harris
    3-16, Repasy 2-33 and 1 touchdown, Young
    2-14, Gilmore 1-6,
East Carolina: Croisetiera 2-19, Wallace 1-16,
    Gordon 1-10, Gianniean 1-4.

TACKLES-ASSISTS
Marshall: Stainback 9-13, L. Brown 7-11,
    Shannon 5-7, Reese 2-9, Sanders 7-3,
    Cottrell 6-2, T. Brown 6-2, Griffith 4-4,
    VanHorn 4-2.
East Carolina: Rothrock 2-10, Mills 6-5,
    Britton 7-3, Peeler 6-3, Zadnick 4-5.

***THE SEASON'S FINAL GAME,
    SCHEDULED FOR SATURDAY, NOV.
    21, 1970, AT OHIO UNIVERSITY IN
    ATHENS, OHIO, WAS CANCELED.***

MARSHALL TEAM, COACHES, FANS
DIE IN PLANE CRASH

75 BELIEVED ABOARD PLANE; AIRLINE SILENT

A chartered jet airliner carrying the Marshall University football team, coaches and a number of prominent Huntington residents crashed in flames on its approach to Tri-State Airport Saturday evening.

There were no survivors.

Southern Airways of Atlanta, Ga., said its two-engine DC-9 was carrying 70 passengers and five crewmen.

The plane was returning the Marshall football players, most of the coaching staff and a group of supporters from Greenville, N.C., where East Carolina University defeated the Marshall team Saturday afternoon.

The crash occurred about 7:45 p.m. less than a mile west of Tri-State Airport. Weather conditions were poor and light rain was falling.

The Herald-Advertiser's Jack Hardin, the first reporter on the scene some 250 yards east of W.Va. 75 south of Kenova, said:

"There's nothing here but charred bodies. It's terrible."

Bodies and wreckage were scattered over a wide area.

Gov. Arch A. Moore Jr. and Dr. Donald N. Dedmon, Marshall's acting president, rushed to the scene.

Hardin reported a piece of the plane was found on a hillside about a half-mile from the principal crash site. He said sections of bodies were reported found there, too. Searchers were combing the hillside early this morning with the aid of flares.

At 12:10 a.m., the first bodies were placed on National Guard trucks. They were being taken to the National Guard Armory at the airport, where a temporary morgue was established. Hardin said recovery crews were running short of bags to hold the bodies.

Southern Airways of Atlanta said it did not have a passenger list, and refused to identify the crewmen pending notification of next of kin.

The tragedy was "the worst domestic air crash this year," a Federal Aviation Agency spokesman in Washington said, and it was described as one of the worst in history involving an athletic team.

The crash also was the worst in West Virginia air travel history.

Charles Dodrill, president of Tri-State Airport Authority, said if the plane were in its normal approach pattern coming into the airport, it would have had its nose slightly up, traveling at a speed of about 160 miles an hour at the point where it crashed.

A nearby resident, Mrs. Larry Bailey of 1926 Coal Branch Road, told Hardin she saw the jet coming down. She said she heard an explosion and "the plane seemed to come down flat."

The Herald-Advertiser's David A. Peyton reported by radio-telephone that he had walked completely around the scene and "everything is charred beyond belief."

Peyton said it appeared an area about 200 feet in diameter had been leveled and small fires were still burning. He said only the plane's two jet engines and a section of wing were recognizable. "Wreckage is scattered [all] over the place. People who were heard [when] it happened said they heard one big 'thud' and that was all."

The heat from the wreckage was hampering recovery efforts. The scene was described as chaotic. Great numbers of people swarmed through thick underbrush to reach the scene during the first two hours. State police were clearing everybody, including newsmen, from the area by 10 p.m.

A Tri-State Airport employee returning from the scene said, "Bodies are stacked in a big heap, all of them charred. There can't be anyone alive."

Police said every ambulance within a 10-mile radius was alerted. Cabell-Huntington Hospital asked visitors to leave, and sealed off its entrances in gearing for the emergency, but it soon became apparent there would be no survivors.

Members of Ceredo and Kenova volunteer fire departments sift through the wreckage from the DC-9 Southern Airlines charter that crashed November 14, 1970, killing all 75 aboard. Passengers included most coaches and players on the 1970 Marshall University football team and a group of supporters returning from a game against East Carolina.

Hardin and Peyton described the scene as horrifying. "There are charred pieces of bodies all over the place," Hardin said. Peyton said he had counted 12 forms that were recognizable as bodies, but that he saw pieces of bodies, bones and limbs scattered throughout the area.

Many of the bodies had been covered with white plastic by firemen and other emergency authorities at the scene.

Gov. Moore arrived at the scene shortly after 10 p.m.

A ten-man investigative team from the National Transportation Safety Board was dispatched from Washington late Saturday night, according to board chairman John H. Reed.

Less than two months ago, on Oct. 3, one of two chartered planes carrying the Wichita [State] University football team, coaches, boosters and others, crashed in the mountains of Colorado, killing 31 persons, including 13 football players.

Traffic was being turned away from the airport at the foot of the road leading up the hill to the terminal.

Southern Airways released a statement at 10:20 p.m. indicating there were 70 passengers aboard. Southern said it was the first crash in its 21 years of operation.

Fifteen bodies were found near a section of the fuselage—the biggest section of the craft left intact.

Searchers combed the area day and night, using flares by night and working in muddy conditions caused by a light snowfall and rain.

The spectacular crash occurred about one and one-fourth mile east of the Kenova exit of Interstate-64 and large numbers of people were drawn to the scene.

Rev. Homer Pelfrey, a former Wayne County sheriff, said he and Floyd Nichols, a resident of the area, were in their homes when they heard the explosion and were the first to arrive on the scene. Mr. Pelfrey said he found a billfold belonging to one of the Marshall players.

State police said the wreckage was still too hot to permit full recovery operations.

An emergency center was established in the office of John Callebs, Marshall director of development, and a group of local ministers had been assembled to notify relatives of victims as soon as positive identification was made.

Gov. Moore spoke with members of families of the victims who had gathered at the airport. He advised them not to go to the temporary morgue because of "the condition of the bodies." The governor then went to the morgue himself.

Marshall officials said the school's cheerleaders were not aboard the plane.

Marshall students were helping to set up temporary quarters for relatives of the victims at Gullickson Hall—the Marshall physical education building. Students were carrying mattresses, pillows and sheets and blankets to the building. Area restaurants were supplying food and coffee.

John Young, who lives about a half-mile from the crash site, said he "heard this loud noise … I ran out to see what it was and all I saw was a big ball of fire. Nobody could have survived that."

Albert Rich, whose house also is about a half mile from the scene, said he first thought the loud noise was lightning. He went out to see.

"I heard this one bang and a minute later there was this terrific bang which shook the whole house. I ran outside to see if there was a storm, and I saw this flash over the hill," Rich said.

He said the plane skimmed the top of an abandoned house before it crashed.

A light rain hampered rescue efforts, where the site was accessible only by a narrow, dirt road which had turned mostly into mud.

It was the second fatal crash at the airport in 16 days. Three Army officers were killed in the crash of a military plane Oct. 29. A fourth passenger, critically injured, survived.

In the earlier crash, the airplane hit a hill 2,700 feet short of the runway, after apparently losing power in one of its two engines.

Military authorities still are investigating the incident.

Approximately 175-200 National Guardsmen were at the airport awaiting instructions. The bulk of the troops, from the 19th Special Forces, returned from field exercises in the Martha area.

Also there were elements of the 254th Transportation Co., which was at the armory when the alert was sounded: the 145th Medical detachment, a helicopter ambulance group, and a detail from Fort Bragg, N.C., who was conducting the weekend maneuvers for the Special Forces at Martha.

Huntington Mayor Robert Hinerman declared a period of mourning until further notice, and requested that all flags over city buildings be flown at half-staff. He asked the public to do the same.

Accompanying him were City Manager Edward Ewing and Gary Bunn, planning director.

City Manager Edward A. Ewing, Mayor Robert Hinerman, and Councilman Owen Duncan, arrived at the airport around 11:30 p.m.

Councilman Duncan said he almost went on the trip. The plane left the airport about 7:30 p.m. Friday.

He said he was just returning from a business trip in Green Bay, Wis., and was leaving the airport when City Councilman Murill Ralsten invited him to go along. Ralsten explained to him the $50 ticket would buy a round trip, one meal, lodging and entrance to the football game.

"I came within a hair of going," Duncan said, adding his sympathies to the families.

A Southern Airways DC-9, apparently exactly like the one which crashed, arrived at Tri-State at 11:50 p.m., carrying a team of investigators for the airline. There were six people aboard the big plane and all made an obvious effort to avoid newsmen. The plane landed from the east, the opposite direction from the attempted landing of the ill-fated Marshall charter plane.

Piedmont Flight 919, the first airplane to land at the airport since the accident, arrived approximately on schedule shortly after midnight.

Stan Champer, one of the passengers on the plane and city editor of the Ashland Daily Independent, said he was originally on a flight from Chicago which was due to land in Huntington at 8:30 p.m.

The passengers were told they would be flying to Roanoke instead of Huntington, Mr. Champer said. At Roanoke the passengers were taken off the Piedmont jet and placed on a Piedmont prop jet for the flight which stopped at Greenbrier Airport, Beckley Airport and Charleston's Kanawha Airport. They arrived four hours late.

Mr. Champer said they were never officially told of the disaster near Huntington. "We thought we were flying over because of bad weather," Mr. Champer said, "but while we were in Roanoke word of the tragedy spread among the passengers quickly."

Mr. Champer was returning from the National Convention of Sigma Delta Chi held last week in Chicago.

Gov. Moore announced early this morning a concurrent investigation would be conducted by state and federal authorities. Airport manager A.O. Cappadony said at 1 a.m. that FAA investigators were expected to arrive in about 45 minutes. Peyton reported that four ambulances had gone to the temporary morgue by 1 a.m.

Cabell County Sheriff Joe Neal, returning to the airport from an inspection of the temporary morgue at the armory, said it was his understanding some bodies were thrown clear of the wreckage and they were identifiable by sight.

He said the National Guard had spread sheets on the floor in preparation for the bodies which he said would probably be brought in in plastic bags. He also said he understood that a cooling unit from the Logan Packing Co. would be brought in to preserve the bodies.

Capt. J.D. Baisden, Company B State Police commander at South Charleston, said no newsmen would be allowed at the temporary morgue until positive identification was made.

Relatives or friends who might give identifications were being allowed within the morgue.

Operations at the airport remained normal and there was to be no interruption of regular flights, officials said.

The damaged fuselage shows the destruction caused when the 95-seat jetliner clipped a tree 66 feet above the ground on a hillside near Tri-State Airport.

TRAGEDY OF HIGHEST DEGREE

By Jack Hardin, The Herald-Advertiser

Gov. Arch A. Moore Jr. stood at the scene and listened as names of non-team members were read to him.

"No … Oh, God. No. This can't be happening. Why do these things have to happen? These people are our friends."

The state's chief executive, after leaving the scene, said it would probably be eight or nine hours before the bodies can be taken. Not until daybreak can a thorough search be conducted.

Special identification teams from the State Police in Charleston are en route to the scene, the governor said, and they will conduct investigation processes on the bodies.

"All that have been found are burned beyond recognition," he said. The bodies will be removed to an airport hangar, and National Guard trucks and other emergency vehicles were available to transfer the bodies.

The governor said some reports indicated the plane hit a hillside west of the runway, bounced off and exploded in mid-air before crashing.

Other reports said the plane first exploded, then hit the hillside, bounced into the air and then crashed.

Harry Hatten, who owns a farm on the other side of the hill, and his family were out in the barnyard at the time of the crash, and saw the plane and remarked, "It's flying too low."

They then saw a flash of fire.

'SONS OF MARSHALL' THEY WILL ALWAYS BE

By David S. McGuire, The Herald-Advertiser

The chartered bus, striped prominently with its bright green, stood empty, still and useless.

The night, befittingly, was miserable.

A chilly wind swept first a drizzle, then a steady rain and finally a few drops on the bus, parked in front of the operations building at Tri-State Airport.

Grimly but efficiently, airport personnel went about their work.

At first there was bewilderment at word of the crash. Then the terrible shock. Finally the incomprehensible grief that overshadows nearly everything when the "Why?" can't be answered.

Authorities called waiting relatives and friends into a room off the terminal lobby and later took families and relatives to the West Virginia Air National Guard Armory, where a temporary morgue was set up in the hangar.

Strict security measures were imposed.

All incoming highway traffic was stopped. Those without official business were not allowed to turn off Walker Branch Road onto the airport road. Only law enforcement officers, National Guardsmen, relatives and others having official business were allowed to take the road leading from the terminal building to the Armory.

A coed wearing a white jacket with the green Marshall University lettering on back walked toward the bank of four pay phones which were all busy. She stopped, turned away, retraced her step and stopped against a pole. Red-eyed and weeping, she bit her fingers and waited her turn.

A few Marshall students wearing fraternity jackets hunched in their chairs while cradling their faces. One had tears streaming down his face.

On the walkway between the terminal and the gates, a cluster of people stood talking in hushed tones.

The tower building was a maze of activity, although traffic into the port was canceled.

One passerby ducked into the ground floor of the tower and flatly said, "Yes, I was over there. Bodies are stacked over there in one big heap, all charred. There can't be anyone alive."

Charles Dodrill, Airport Authority president, was busy in the operations building talking on a telephone. "No, there isn't anything official yet," he commented at 9:35 p.m. "Word of the casualties, of course, will have to come from Southern Airways," he answered.

Moments later, word came that state police said there were no survivors.

Outside, the rain picked up in tempo and the wind felt chillier, much chillier.

And there was the bus, idling after the driver became cold. Idling almost like a drum roll in slow motion.

Soon, the driver reappeared and asked if he were free to go. "An Army officer told me to stand by in case there were any survivors. I called the office and they said for me to shuttle survivors to the hospital," he explained.

"Well, in that case, you are free to go," he was told.

Silently, he turned and walked toward the bus.

The almost military cadence of the engine brought to mind the Marshall Fight Song.

There were no Sons of Marshall aboard when the green-striped bus pulled slowly away.

Nevertheless, there were truly Sons of Marshall. Gone, yes, but still Sons of Marshall.

THE TRAGEDY

By Ernie Salvatore, The Herald-Advertiser

What do you write at a time like this?

You believe that it can never really happen to your own people. Others go down in air crashes. Entire teams are wiped out. Individuals with well known names go down in their isolated tragedies and you mourn briefly for their misfortune.

But, never to your own people.

Then, it comes into the news room, silently, swiftly, it comes—a simple report that a chartered airliner carrying the Marshall University football team home from its ninth game of the season has crashed against a soggy West Virginia hillside, two miles short of the runway.

And, the report says, it immediately exploded into flames.

"Ambulances are requested from all points in the area," the police radio crackles.

You can't believe it. Twenty-five years in the newspaper business notwithstanding, you can't believe it. But soon, the mounting truth of it all forces you to believe it. There is nothing else you can do.

REPORTS INCLUDE FRIENDS NAMES

The first fragmentary reports include the names of your friends. Coaches, athletic department people, players, just plain loyal friends who went where the Thundering Herd went in all kinds of weather, under all kinds of conditions, win, lose or draw.

Incredible. Less than two months ago a large portion of the Wichita State team was wiped out in a similar tragedy.

Now, it's our own beloved Marshall.

Who'll be next? How many more tragedies of this kind are going to occur before a way is found to stop them?

An honest question, asked in grief, and it deserves an honest, straightforward answer. Fatalism has no place in these circumstances; at least that is what you tell yourself.

The Marshall air tragedy is the worst in the history of West Virginia. It is the third involving a college football team within the past decade, the second indirectly involving a Mid-American Conference team, indirectly because Marshall no longer is a member of that athletic body but was for 18 years. The first involved the California

Poly team on a takeoff tragedy at the Toledo Airport after it had played Bowling Green, a MAC member.

This is the sum and the substance [of] the crash.

PERHAPS THE FINAL CHAPTER

And, in that blinding explosion, another and perhaps the final chapter in the worst era in Marshall athletics has been written.

It began with the athletic recruiting scandal that hit the campus in 1969. It continued with the suspension from the Mid-American Conference, and the almost total overhaul of the athletic department. Probation from the National Collegiate Athletic Association of one year's duration followed.

Though an application for readmittance to the Mid-American was denied last February, the tides began to shift in Marshall's favor. Money was allocated by the state to remodel Fairfield Stadium, cover it with AstroTurf, and improve other facilities on the campus.

An ambitious fund raising drive was launched, aimed at a goal of $150,000, the largest in the school's history. The coaches were brought in. Schedules were being adjusted. The idea was that if Marshall could not find a family of schools to belong to, it would operate as a full-grown independent.

The year's football team was to take the first step in that direction. Consisting of holdovers from last year's Thundering Herd which, along with the scandals, had to suffer through a winless streak that reached 27 games before ending with a three-game winning streak, it got off to a good start.

But, injuries to the thin forces, never numbering more than 48 players in this age of specialization, took their toll. Nevertheless, except for losses to Toledo and Western Michigan, the Herd was in contention in every game it played.

The team locker room in the basement of Gullickson Hall, November 20 1970.

WON THREE LOST SIX

When the end came against that hillside Saturday night, it had won three games, and lost six—two by three points, and one by two points. Always against superior forces. Always against the odds. That seemed to be this ball club's luck. That seemed to be Marshall's luck in recent years.

There was a touch of irony in Greenville, N.C., Saturday where Marshall bowed to East Carolina before emplaning on its ill-fated trip. Watching his old school for the first time since his graduation in 1935 was one of the greatest football players in Marshall history, John Zontini, "The Sheik of Seth."

Last week Zontini was elected to the West Virginia Sports Hall of Fame. The entire 1970 Marshall team should be inducted with him next spring in Morgantown along with those people who went down with it.

These deaths have to be given some kind of meaning. Perhaps there will be one in this gesture.

Fairfield Stadium, home to the Thundering Herd for 62 years, was a place for prayerful reflections on November 15 1970.

NATIONAL GUARD VETERAN CAN NEVER FORGET THAT NIGHT

By Bob Withers, The Herald-Dispatch

Thirty-five years later, memories of the Marshall University plane crash are still too nightmarish for 71-year-old Gary Bunn as he surveys the site of the disaster in a gulley between U.S. 52 and Coal Branch Road near Kenova. Bunn was commander of a National Guard unit that was placed on state duty to help with the clean-up, victim identification and perimeter security.

HUNTINGTON—Gary Bunn never has forgotten that night. He's afraid he never will.

The 71-year-old Huntington man was the city's planning director when 75 Marshall University players, coaches and fans died in a plane crash as they returned to Tri-State Airport in 1970. He also was commander of Company B, 2nd Battalion, 19th Special Forces Group, of the West Virginia Army National Guard.

In fact, that's what saved him from being on the doomed plane. And it's also what handed him an up-close-and-personal look at the horror he had avoided.

Actually, he hasn't escaped some of the trauma. You can see it in his face when he revisits the crash site - as he did in 2005.

"I still have nightmares," he said softly.

City Councilman Murrill Ralsten had invited Bunn and his wife Nancy to fly on the chartered jet to the Marshall-East Carolina University game at Greenville, N.C., when he stopped in Ralsten's shop to buy a tie and belt. But when Bunn got home, his wife reminded him that he had a drill that weekend.

"The National Guard saved our lives," Bunn said.

On that fateful Saturday, a Special Forces team from Fort Bragg, N.C., came up to conduct some airborne operations with Company B, and the two units scheduled a jump at DZ-Guyan, near the Esquire Country Club. But when Bunn, who served as jumpmaster, stuck his head out the door of the C-119 in which they were flying and saw it was pouring rain, he aborted the jump.

That evening, he told his troops they would try the jump again on Sunday and sent them back out to Barboursville for night maneuvers. When Bunn got home, his wife met him at the door.

"Something terrible just happened at the airport," she said. "A big plane has crashed."

Bunn returned immediately. His troops already had driven a deuce-and-a-half full of stretchers to the crash site in a hollow between the Tolsia Highway (now U.S. 52) and Coal Branch Road, expecting to find survivors.

The descending Southern Airways DC-9, flying eastward toward the runway, was much lower than it should have been on that damp, foggy evening, the National Transportation Safety Board later concluded. At about 7:35 p.m., its wings and wheels struck several trees on a high hill west of the highway and cut a sickening swath through them for hundreds of feet. The jet rolled, inverted and plunged nose-first into the gulley, exploding on impact. All in about five seconds.

"The heat was so intense, you couldn't get closer than 100 yards," Bunn said. "It burned for a day or two. It's unreal where it ended up, isn't it?"

Still not sure what the burning wreckage was, Bunn drove up to the armory. At that point, there were "rumors" it was the Marshall plane.

"I turned numb and sick to my stomach," he said. "Nancy and I could have been on that thing."

About two hours later, Gov. Arch A. Moore Jr. and State Police Supt. Fred Donohoe showed up, and the governor placed several members of Company B on state active duty to help with recovery, victim identification and security. Guardsmen were bringing human remains into the armory in garbage bags - there were no body bags

Gary Bunn.

available until Walter "Lefty" Rollins brought several from Rollins Funeral Home.

"I identified a lot of people myself," Bunn said. "Some bodies weren't burned. I remember a tackle who had been thrown out of the plane; he had tree limbs all through his body. After that, our guys started looking around all over the woods to see if anybody survived."

As the days and nights dragged on, the Guard worked with the FBI and a forensics team from Wright-Patterson Air Force Base. Except for one brief respite to go home and change uniforms—"I threw the old one in the garbage"—Bunn stayed at the armory for a week, 24/7.

"It was morbid," he said. "We used I-don't-know-how-many gallons of disinfectant and preserving powder. "It still gives me cold chills."

The longer Bunn stared at the crash site, the more memories surfaced.

"Part of our mission was security, keeping people away from the crash scene and the armory, which we had turned into a temporary morgue," he said. "One day we caught a photographer from a national magazine on top of the water tower, trying to shoot all those bodies through the windows on top of the armory."

Bunn, enraged, ordered prompt and decisive action.

"Tell that guy he has about five seconds to get down, or we'll bring him down with a bullet," he told his troops.

In the years since, Bunn has wrestled with guilt because he escaped the flight that doomed many of his personal friends.

"I should have been on that plane," he said. "It goes through your mind all the time. I wake up sometimes in a cold sweat."

Bunn mentioned a couple of his men, who later added their own memories to that night's tragic tapestry. Take, for example, Ron Rutherford, 75, of Culloden, who was a sergeant major in Company B at the time.

"I was in combat in Korea for over a year, and I never saw anything worse," he said.

Rutherford said he was alone at the armory when the plane crashed. He heard a sound, but thought it was a plane breaking the sound barrier. The first inkling he had of the true nature of the tragedy hit him when he got a call from a national newscaster in New York.

That's about the time Marion Priestly, 70, of Huntington, who lived in Cincinnati at the time, drove in for the drill late. Rutherford dispatched him to walk up to the tower and see what had happened.

"I saw the Marshall bus waiting," said Priestly, who was a master sergeant then.

"The driver was worried. They were supposed to be in by then, and he had heard a noise and saw a flash."

Confirming the worst in the tower, Priestly hurried back to the armory and Rutherford sent him out to Barboursville to bring back the troops on maneuvers. Priestly had returned by the time they started bringing in the bodies.

"You couldn't recognize anything," he said. "It's an unforgettable thing."

After Bunn had thoroughly looked over the crash site, he climbed back in his Ford Explorer and rubbed his chin with his hand. He sat there for a few moments, pensive, seeming reluctant to leave.

"Oh boy," he muttered, and turned on the ignition.

COMMUNITY MEMBERS REMEMBER 1970

Different generations have different disasters etched into their memories. Many remember where they were when they heard of President Kennedy's assassination, or who was with them when the space shuttle Challenger exploded, or what they were doing when the news of the 9/11 terrorist attacks reached them. For those connected to Huntington, the night of November 14, 1970, holds a similar place.

For some, the memories come to the forefront in November of each year. Others have been called up when the people viewed "Ashes to Glory," a documentary of the plane crash and the subsequent rebirth and rise of Marshall football, released around the 30th anniversary. These accounts, related by people with different connections to the tragedy, have appeared in The Herald-Dispatch over the years.

FORMER ASSISTANT MARSHALL COACH CARL KOKOR

Carl Kokor was an assistant coach for the Herd in 1970. He missed the flight from East Carolina to Huntington because he was scouting Ohio University in its game at Penn State. Marshall was scheduled to play Ohio the following week.

Kokor said at the 2000 memorial that the crash remains in his life as "a drive, an additional gear." When he saw "Ashes to Glory" Sunday, he thought of a different, more appropriate title.

"Glory from Ashes," Kokor said. "The glory is now. It came from the ashes."

FORMER HERALD-DISPATCH SPORTS WRITER LOWELL CADE

Former sports reporter Lowell Cade, who retired in 1997, said he could have been on the plane.

"Mike Brown and I split up covering Marshall on the road," he said. "It just so happened that I chose to go to Bowling Green and Toledo. Mike covered the East Carolina game."

Ironically, Brown also chose to drive to Greenville, N.C., with his wife instead of taking the team plane. Cade was on the sports desk the night of the crash and received a call from veteran police reporter Jack Hardin.

"He asked me if I knew someone named John Young,"

So devastated were community members that even hospital workers needed to take time for a memorial service at St. Mary's Hospital two days after the crash.

Cade said. "I told him that he was a tight end on Marshall's team.

"That's when we realized that the Marshall plane had crashed. It was a terrible night."

WSAZ-TV NEWS ANCHOR BOS JOHNSON

Bos Johnson, the longtime WSAZ-TV news anchor, says the Marshall plane crash was by far the "saddest" news story of his eventful career.

"I was off that night when I heard a news flash about a plane crash at the airport," Johnson told The Herald-Dispatch in November 1999. "I thought that it had to be the Marshall plane because of the time. I remember going in and being on the air past midnight.

"I don't really understand how I was able to do it now. Nothing has had more of an impact on this community. Dottie (his wife) and I attended 13 funerals in a week. I still get teary-eyed when I see the children of some of the victims I knew."

COMMUNITY MEMBER CAROLYN R. BARR

"One could not watch 'Ashes to Glory' without being touched," Carolyn R. Barr wrote to The Herald-Dispatch in November 2000. "Looking into the faces of those featured, one could see the past, the present and the future.

"Some things arrive in their own mysterious hour, on their own terms and not yours. The Marshall University plane crash affected many who were never acknowledged or credited for their participation in this piece of history.

"First to arrive on the scene were the West Virginia State Police, who organized the rest of the law enforcement agencies and fire departments. They continued working nonstop to secure the area and begin the recovery effort. Those involved in that effort are the silent ones - they never spoke, nor were asked about something that touched their lives so immensely.

"I've often wondered why nothing is ever written of those who gave so much of themselves. Their knowledge and memories would be invaluable. But the important

Crowd gathers at Veterans Memorial Field House for services the day after the Marshall football team's chartered airliner crashed.

part is to acknowledge their involvement. One of those is the father of my two daughters. He seldom speaks of the event, but I cannot help but remember his emotions at that time - in the form of silence and grief.

"I would like to acknowledge those who have remained so silent but gave so much. They are tomorrow's past."

COMMUNITY MEMBER GARY KLINE

"November in Huntington is such a peaceful time," Gary Kline of Ona wrote to The Herald-Dispatch in November 2003. "The tree-lined streets and stately two-story brick homes lend a quiet character to this town. November is also a sad time for this community, as well. Those who have lost someone close probably understand the emptiness that can remain for years after their loss. For this reason, it is understandable how this community still mourns the loss of their adoptive sons and daughters in a tragic event that still scars the souls of each and every person that calls Huntington home.

"Marshall football is more than a game. It is, rather, a living testament to the spirit of humankind. Sometimes, the stark realities of life will extinguish the

Members of the Marshall University band during a memorial service at Veterans Memorial Field House November 15, 1970.

flame of youth and hope, like it did on a cold rainy night on a dark Wayne County hillside. What is unknown by nature, is that this spirit, seemingly extinguished in a blazing mass of twisted metal and dreams interrupted, is now glowing like a beacon to those who have lost hope. This beacon guides them through the difficulties of life, giving course and direction. From those smoldering embers burn the hope of the next generation.

"Those who follow Marshall football are among the most aware of what being a fan is really about. They understand that it goes beyond the game. The very nature of this understanding is the fuel that powers this program to the height that it has reached. It will be this very understanding that will power this program to a height not yet realized. Perspective can sometimes be sobering when viewing football as merely a game. We appear quite childish, if indeed that's all there is to our discipleship. But we know better don't we? It's more than that.

"The masses that pass beneath the memorial bronze at the stadium will feel the cold November breeze on their faces. With a sad smile, they push on, knowing that those outside the circle of Herd Nation really do not understand. This symbol of unconquerable spirit reminds us that in life, good things don't come easy. It reminds us that Marshall football means more than what a gathering of our most God blessed and physically gifted young members of society accomplish on a given day. Marshall football is the conquering of fear and doubt. It is overcoming overwhelming odds.

"On game days in Huntington, the stadium will fill with anticipation. The old timers, still amazed at the lofty climb, look around at the young becoming part of the indoctrination. And high atop a nearby hill in Spring Hill Cemetery stands the marker above the grave of a spirit that just wouldn't die. And through the quiet of this peaceful setting resonates the sound of 'We are ... Marshall.'"

COMMUNITY MEMBER ROGER A. HESSON

"On the evening of Saturday, Nov. 14, 1970, my wife and I had a living room full of neighbors waiting for Marshall's assistant football coach Frank Loria to get home from East Carolina," Roger A. Hesson of Barboursville wrote to The Herald-Dispatch. "He was to get home about 9 p.m., bring his wife and two little girls across the street to my house, sing happy birthday to Bernice, help cut the cake and enjoy his friends after a hard road trip.

"A message came across the TV screen providing the terrible news. Bernice and I rushed across the street to be with Phyllis Loria, who was expecting another child the next month. When we arrived at her door, her phone rang, and she at that moment

The community looked for spiritual help in coping with the devastation in the aftermath of the crash, including services at St. Mary's Hospital, Veterans Memorial Field House and the Campus Christian Center.

received the news of Frank's death.

"Frank played in the Hula Bowl when he was an All-American defensive back for Virginia Tech. Frank was a very competitive person. It was ironic that he had moved into the residence of former Marshall football coach Perry Moss. The two had never met.

"I was director of payroll at Marshall at this time. Many trips were made by me to the Wayne County Coroners Office securing death certificates as they were processed. I will always remember the funerals and funeral home visits to say farewell to my many friends and co-workers."

COMMUNITY MEMBER DAVE MARCUM

"It was raining on that Saturday in November in Greensburg, Pa., a typical football Saturday around home, too rainy for golf so watching football on TV was the order of the day," writes Dave Marcum of Huntington. "After dinner, it was back to the TV to watch the late games.

"News break, CBS News - a plane carrying Marshall University's football team has crashed while attempting a right-turn landing at Huntington, W.Va., Tri-State Airport.

"I got up from my chair and grabbed my car keys.

"Lots of churches, lots of funerals, my last memory was holding onto the chain link fence at the south end of Fairfield Stadium, staring through the fence at a black wreath that had been laid on the 50-yard line.

"I must have been there for a long time staring and crying. An old man who lived across from where I stood came and touched my shoulder and said, "You can look for as long as you like, but they ain't never coming back. If you have a family, you need to go to them and get on with your life" - and so I did.

MARSHALL TEACHER
ELIZABETH HINES CZOMPO

"On a rainy, gloomy evening 33 years ago, my husband and I were coming back to town from our place in Wayne County," wrote Elizabeth Hines Czompo of Huntington. "When we reached the house, we unloaded quickly, ate a snack and turned on the television. An announcement came about a plane accident near the airport.

"I wasn't paying much attention - probably looking at mail or newspapers - then it caught my attention. The news was probably about Marshall's plane. It would be returning from the game about this time.

"I screamed to my husband who was in another room, "Did you hear that? I think Marshall's plane has crashed!"

"About an hour earlier, we were driving on the road the plane crossed just before crashing. I think I was in some kind of shock. I almost feel it now.

"There must be several pieces of wood from the plane hidden in memory vaults, as we heard the next day that people were going to the crash site for pieces of the plane.

"At this time, I was teaching at Marshall. I lost several students. There were black wreaths at public buildings. I remember the one at City Hall because it was very large and gave me a strange feeling.

"I missed my students."

The community turned to prayer during memorial services in the days following the plane crash.

Words cannot describe the numbness that was felt in the community in the days following the Marshall tragedy.

JOHN AND ELAINE WHITFIELD

George and Bonnie Wallace of Rainelle, W.Va., wrote to The Herald-Dispatch in November 2005 to tell about John and Elaine Whitfield.

"They became designated ancillary guardians of Charles and Rachael Arnold's daughters eight months after the couple was killed in the plane crash," they write. "This couple will be rewarded someday in heaven for keeping these four girls together and raising them with their one daughter, Missy. They had to have a heart of gold to take on this task of raising this many girls.

"We met these folks while living in Huntington back in 1994 to 1997. I just wanted others to know what great people John and Elaine are."

FACULTY WIVES, OTHERS HELPED AFTER CRASH

"The fateful airplane crash on Saturday evening, Nov. 14, 1970, produced a substantial number of unsung heroes," William P. Stephenson of Huntington wrote to The Herald-Dispatch in November 2005.

"The Marshall University Faculty Wives Association was an example of those persons who mobilized to assist.

"At that time, Jean Modlin was president of the group. Within an hour of hearing of the crash, which took the lives of 75 Marshall team members and supporters, Mrs. Modlin and others in the group were organizing their fellow members into family assistance teams, with the acumen only experienced wives and mothers could have.

"Members were soon visiting and comforting bereaved parents, wives and children. Emergency meals and foods were prepared and delivered to households. Assistance was given to help with those tasks which occur with shock of sudden deaths.

"Monetary contributions were also made to the Faculty Wives. Most of the contributions became part of the nucleus of the funds that were pledged for the construction of the Marshall memorial.

"The Faculty Wives continued their assistance for an extended length of time. As an example, a number of children who lost a parent in the tragedy hopefully had a happier Christmas.

"There were other groups and persons, along with the Faculty Wives, who answered the call to assist. In general, these unsung heroes received no accolades. Nor did they ask for such. When they heard the call, they were there to help."

KENOVA RESIDENT JEAN BAILEY

Jean Bailey remembers it like it was yesterday - an enormous jet plane falling toward her Kenova-area home.

Spellbound, she watched from her kitchen window, fearing the aircraft would crash directly into her house, which she shared that damp, gloomy Saturday evening with her husband and their two young sons.

"It sounded like popcorn popping, and I thought, 'What was that?'" she told The Herald-Dispatch in November 2005. "It looked like it was coming straight toward our house. It was breaking off trees when it hit. It hit right around the road from us.

"The devastating thing was I just knew who that was (aboard)."

FORMER ACTING MARSHALL UNIVERSITY PRESIDENT SAM CLAGG

Sam Clagg, a former acting Marshall University president, was chairman of Marshall's geography department and president of the university council when the crash occurred on his 50th birthday. He was instrumental in coordinating faculty and students during the aftermath, as well as helping identify victims and selecting a memorial site at Spring Hill Cemetery where six unidentified players are buried.

"Anytime you have an ailment, you have scar tissue," he said in November 2005. "Never does that day go by that I don't give it a thought."

Clagg said the crash, however, unified Marshall and the Huntington community in a way that's impossible to comprehend three and a half decades later.

"I'm a great believer in the fact that time solves every problem," he said. "Through the years, we have forgotten the horrendous portions of it and remembered the goodness that may have been in it. Above all, the magnificence of the people involved should be remembered."

MORTUARY OWNER BOB CARPENTER

Bob Carpenter of Klingel-Carpenter Mortuary in Huntington said that sense of togetherness was something special - even in a profession accustomed to death and grieving.

"Everyone pulled together in a very strong way," he said in November 2005. "This is what made it so unusual and so unique. ... You see one or two (deaths), but you don't see 75."

Marshall students remember their teammates at a memorial wall in Old Main in November 1970.

Carpenter also was instrumental in helping during the crash aftermath. He even was approached by the National Funeral Directors Association to help communities throughout the U.S. deal with disasters resulting in widespread death - something he did during the 1970s and 1980s.

MORTUARY OWNER LUCY ROLLINS

Lucy Rollins, whose family operates Rollins Funeral Home in Kenova, vividly remembers where she was the foggy, rainy evening of Nov. 14, 1970. A call from a family member shattered a quiet night at a Gallipolis, Ohio, motel with family and friends.

"That put a black cloud over us," she said in November 2005. "We went down to eat, but we couldn't really eat."

Rollins' family, including her late brother-in-law Walter "Lefty" Rollins Jr., also were heavily involved in the recovery effort. The Federal Aviation Administration requested their help, and Walter Rollins, a coroner, helped identify many of the victims' remains.

Lucy Rollins said the emotional impact of the crash has resonated throughout the Tri-State and beyond for many reasons. Most prominently, she said, the crash occurred practically in local residents' back yards and took the lives of so many people in their prime, including physicians, a dentist, a City Council member and a well-known local car dealer.

"It was such a tragic accident, and life goes on," Lucy Rollins said. "You never forget something like that. You never forget death, but you learn you can't do anything about it, and you keep going."

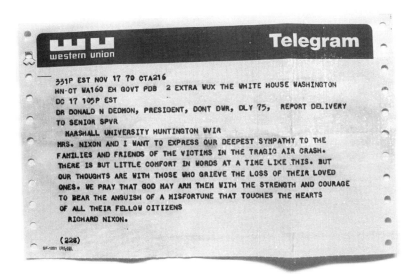

President Richard M. Nixon offers his thoughts and prayers following the crash. Later, in 1971, Nixon offered congratulations to the 1971 young Herd saying, "Whatever the season brings, you have already won your greatest victory by putting the 1971 Varsity squad on the field."

FORMER MARSHALL MANAGER REMEMBERS PHONE CALL THAT CHANGED LIFE FOREVER

By David Walsh, The Herald-Dispatch

HUNTINGTON—Eugene Jones remembers the phone call that changed his life.

It was 1970 and the 18-year-old Jones was fresh out of Talcott High School in Summers County, W.Va., and just beginning his freshman year at Marshall University as a student equipment manager for the football team under a work-study program.

On Nov. 14, 1970, the Thundering Herd was scheduled to play East Carolina. Jones talked his way onto the chartered flight that would take players, coaches, athletic department staff and fans to Greenville, N.C. But, on the Tuesday before the game, Jones received news from home about his grandmother's death.

Jones and his sister went home for the funeral. He informed Marshall coaches he would stay through the weekend, meaning he would miss the game and his first flight.

On the trip home from Greenville, where East Carolina defeated Marshall (17-14), the Southern Airways jet crashed short of the runway at Tri-State Airport and all 75 aboard died. At a party at a friend's house that rainy night, Jones heard about the tragedy in a phone call from his father.

The 34th memorial service to remember the victims who died that night is today at 2 p.m. at the fountain outside Memorial Student Center.

Jones won't be at the memorial service, but said he'll take time out, as he always does, to remember his friends. To this day Jones said he's still haunted by one question—why wasn't he on the plane?

"After that day, I began asking the question, 'why not me'?" Jones said Oct. 23 when he returned for Homecoming and watched Marshall's 48-14 victory over Buffalo at Joan C. Edwards Stadium. "I had to fight feelings of guilt. We often don't understand why things happen when they do, but I'm firmly convinced that my life was saved by God and divine intervention. People told me how lucky I was, but I know luck had nothing to do with it."

After the crash, about a week passed before Jones returned to campus.

"I always felt guilty about missing the flight," he said. "I regret not attending funerals, speaking to families who lost loved ones. I just couldn't deal with it. I have always admired Nate Ruffin, Ed Carter (Herd players who missed the trip because of injuries and family matters) and others who became spokesmen for Marshall University and the Marshall survivors."

As time moved on, Jones said he would experience moments when the question about why was he spared would arise. He said he got the answer from a friend one Sunday at church.

"I wondered what my purpose was," he said. "I had my two boys with me. I didn't do anything spectacular. Nate (Ruffin) was the spokesman. Eddie (Carter) was the evangelist. My friend then told me. ... to be their father. I was left to be a husband, a father, a brother, a son (who helps take care of his father who is in a nursing home, and mother who lives alone), a friend to those who need help. I found myself saying yes to things I never imagined myself doing."

During his recent visit Jones also participated in Bring Back the Herd weekend activities for former team managers and athletic trainers.

While a student, Jones worked under Marshall equipment manager John Hagan. Some of the duties during two-a-days involved lining off practice fields on campus, carrying dummies out and having plenty of chin straps ready. When practice shifted to remodeled Fairfield Stadium with its new Astroturf, that meant rides to transport equipment and supplies

And, yes, there was plenty of laundry to be done on a daily basis. Jones said he didn't mind all the work.

"I was spending this much time with players and coaches," he said. "I considered them my friends. Even though I was a manager and not a player, I felt connected to the team. We laughed together at pregame meals, practice and traveling to road games."

Jones said when the players learned he had an older sister in a sorority, he got more attention and requests.

When it came time for the East Carolina game, Jones said funds were limited and only one additional manager could make the trip. That's when he did some serious "begging and pleading" with fellow manager Jerry Seiber, a senior. The two finally agreed Jones would fly and Seiber would bus the next week for the season finale at Ohio University.

"I had never flown before. I was very excited," Jones said in recalling that moment.

The death of his grandmother and the plane crash made all that excitement irrelevant. Once Jones did get back to campus, he had to help unpack the travel bags players had taken to the game. He said the first jersey he pulled out was No. 82 which belonged to wide receiver Jack Repasy.

"There was a little blood on the jersey," he said. "I told myself I can't do this. It was too hard. I left. I regret that decision now."

Some 25 years later, Jones said he received a phone call from someone who wondered if the person he was talking to was indeed Jones. Seiber, the caller, tracked down a phone number for Jones through the Marshall alumni office.

"We relived old times. Jerry said how he'd gone out of town for the weekend, and when he didn't see my name on the passenger list, he didn't know what happened to me," Jones said. Seiber graduated in December 1970 and left Huntington and could only wonder for many years what had happened to Jones.

In 1995, Seiber came down from New Jersey to join Jones, a season-ticket holder, at a Marshall game. They both had kept a practice jersey from 1970 and wore them on special occasions. Seiber has No. 24 and Jones has No. 22.

"We've developed a special bond and friendship that we both share with other Marshall survivors," Jones said. "The bond of Marshall football reaches far and wide."

During ceremonies at the stadium on the 30th anniversary of the crash, Jones said he spent time with former players, especially members of the Young Thundering Herd, and coaches. He said it was special seeing the bronze memorial plaque go up outside the stadium.

Upon returning home that weekend, Jones said he watched "Ashes To Glory," the award-winning documentary about the crash and the struggle to recover from it. During the segment at Fairfield Stadium showing the 30th anniversary memorial service the camera showed some fans.

"Suddenly, there I was, head bowed," Jones said. "My wife said, 'that was you.' I was able to hold it together the rest of the film."

Jones said memories of that day, suppressed for 30 years, came rushing back and tears began to flow. That was minor compared to what happened when he saw the list of players listed one by one on the screen at the end of the film.

"That was the first time I truly broke down," he said. "After 30 years, I cried. I finally had closure."

Jones said this year's Homecoming was special to him, as is the progress made by the football program and university since Nov. 14, 1970.

"It was great to be back and see so many people," he said. "Things are so different and so much bigger. I've never stopped supporting Marshall one bit. The facilities, compared to what the people in our era saw, make you appreciate how far Marshall has come. I heard stories I never heard before.

"I feel so privileged to have been a part of it."

DEPUTY SHERIFF WATCHED IN DISBELIEF AS EVENTS UNFOLDED ON TELEVISION

By David Walsh, The Herald-Dispatch

HUNTINGTON—For Doug Myers, the fitrst bit of news about Marshall football on Nov. 14, 1970 wasn't good. East Carolina defeated the Thundering Herd, 17-14, that afternoon in Greenville, N.C.

The second bit of Marshall football news for Myers, on what had turned into a rainy evening in Huntington, turned out to be devastating.

A Southern Airways chartered jet bringing the team, coaches, athletic department staff and fans back from the game crashed short of the runway at Tri-State Airport in Kenova. There were no survivors in the party of 75.

"I remember watching TV," said Myers, a deputy for the Cabell County Sherriff's Department at the time of the tragedy. "The flash came on. I couldn't believe it. That many lost. I'd flown into the airport before and was scared."

Today, Myers works for Aaron's Products and also operates The Peanut Shoppe in the Huntington Arcade on Fourth Avenue downtown.

As that eventful night went on, Myers remembers seeing footage of law enforcement officials roaming the hillside looking for survivors.

"You're glued to the set, but you can't see much," he said. "You can only hope someone survives. It was so sad. You think about the football players first. They were so young. This community lost a lot of good people, too. Everybody knew somebody who was lost."

Suggestions were made for Marshall to drop football after the crash because the Herd was coming off a recruiting scandal two years earlier (one year probation by the NCAA for 140 violations) and the school last had a winning season in 1964.

Marshall opted to carry on and Myers was happy.

"You hoped they'd play," he said. "You knew it would be a while (to be competitive). You were starting all over."

In the home opener in 1971, the Herd knocked off Xavier, 15-13, with a touchdown on the final play of the game.

"You'd have thought that would've been impossible," he said. "We hung in there no matter what the score was."

Myers and his wife, Donna, were regulars at Fairfield Stadium. When Fairfield Stadium was torn down to make way for Cabell Huntington Hospital medical facilities, Myers collected some bricks. He cleaned one up and presented to his son, Nathan. Another brick, after being cleaned, will be displayed in the Marshall-dominated Peanut Shoppe window. The stained glass window is decorated with MU letters created by another son, Stetson.

Today, the Myers family attends games at Joan C. Edward Stadium.

In 1984, Marshall beat East Tennessee State, 31-28, in the final game of the regular season to finish 6-5 and end the long streak of losing seasons. Since then, the Herd's gone on to dominate in the Southern Conference and Mid-American Conference, had unbeaten seasons, was ranked in the NCAA Division I-A Top 10, traveled to bowl games and produced three Heisman Trophy candidates.

"You hear that cheer, 'We Are Marshall'," Myers said. "You think about 1970 up to now. You get excited."

The plane crash is sure to be featured on newscasts Monday when the school holds the annual memorial service at the Marshall Memorial Student Center.

"I'll stop, watch and remember," Myers said. "We have much to be thankful for."

Doug Myers was a deputy for the Cabell County Sherriff's Department at the time of the tragedy.

SCHOOL ASSIGNMENT KEPT STUDENT ASSISTANT AT HOME

By David Walsh, The Herald-Dispatch

HUNTINGTON—The need to complete a school assignment for graduation meant Joe Wortham couldn't perform a work assignment on Nov. 14, 1970.

At that time, Wortham was a Marshall senior and a student assistant in the sports information office. Gene Morehouse, the sports information director, also did Thundering Herd radio broadcasts, so a student assistant would make football road trips to handle duties in the press box. The 1970 schedule listed Marshall at East Carolina that day and that meant boarding a plane instead of a bus.

Wortham had first choice for road trips, and the East Carolina game was most attractive, but he had to pass because the national teacher's exam he needed to graduate was scheduled that day as well. Student assistant Gary George made the trip instead.

Wortham, 57, now the concessions manager for Marshall athletics, took the exam and headed home to listen to the game on the radio. Marshall lost, 17-14. The chartered Southern Airways jet crashed short of the runway at Tri-State Airport in Kenova on that rainy night and all 75 aboard died, including George and Morehouse, which hit Wortham hard.

"I was flipping through radio channels and heard a news flash (between 7 and 7:30 p.m.) that a DC 9 had crashed," Wortham said. "I knew the schedule and about the time the team was due back. Boom, my heart drops. I make calls to try and get more information. What I feared happened.

"I realized I was plain lucky. At the time (when the football schedule came out), I had a plum and got kind of upset I had to miss it."

Wortham and the rest of the Marshall and Huntington community learned there were no survivors. He volunteered to go to the airport and help identify bodies, but because of the fiery crash, the assignment couldn't be done so he headed home. Later he attended the memorial service at Veterans Memorial Field House.

Shortly after that, interim athetic director Ed Starling named Wortham as the interim sports information director. He had to finish a basketball media guide. A week after the crash, he boarded a plane with the basketball team for a game in New

York. "That wasn't easy," he said. In 1972, Jack Yager became the SID and Wortham moved into the ticket office and eventually became ticket manager.

Wortham lost a lot of friends that day, one of the best being Morehouse.

"He was the sweetest, best person I've ever been associated with," he said. "He always found good in what you did. If you had a paper due, he said take care of the school work first, we'll get the job done. That's the type of person you love to work for."

The school resumed football in 1971 with the team known as the Young Thundering Herd. A long streak of losing seasons ended in 1984 when Marshall went 6-5. Since that time, the program' has enjoyed a continuous ascent.

"You run the gamut of emotion," Wortham said. "From the plane crash in 1970, to 1984 to now. A lot of people tried hard. The commitment level then and now made a difference. When you look at the university, community and state and see what's been done, it amazes me."

TEACHER'S EXAM SAVED BANKSTON

By David Walsh, The Herald-Dispatch

Mike Bankston, who missed the ill-fated trip while a student assistant coach at Marshall in 1970, played the role of an assistant coach in the 2006 Warner Brothers film "We Are Marshall."

ATLANTA—Mike Bankston had an academic conflict that prevented him from being one of the victims of the Nov. 14, 1970, Marshall University plane crash.

Bankston was a student assistant coach for the 1970 Marshall football team working with the freshman squad. On Nov. 13, 1970, the Thundering Herd flew to Greenville, N.C., where it would meet East Carolina the next day. Bankston didn't make the trip because he had to take the National Teacher's Exam. There were no other possible dates.

East Carolina won the game, 17-14. Then the chartered jet bringing the Herd, coaches, athletic department staff and fans home crashed short of the runway at Tri-State Airport in Kenova. All 75 aboard died.

Last week Bankston had a role as a Marshall assistant coach in the movie "We Are Marshall" being filmed in the Atlanta area. The film by Warner Bros. Pictures is an inspirational drama based on the true story of Marshall's and Huntington's efforts to rebuild after the devasting crash.

The movie starts with the East Carolina game and wraps up with the Marshall-Xavier game in 1971. The Young Thundering Herd scores on the final play to beat the Musketeers, 15-13, in its home opener at Fairfield Stadium.

Bankston, 59, lives now in McDonough, Ga., and has strong memories of November 1970.

"It was a tough week," he said, remembering. "I got to say goodbye and good luck to them, but I didn't get to say welcome home."

Bankston's movie scenes were from the Marshall-East Carolina game.

During the week film crews shot game action, the locker room scene after the game, the Marshall party boarding the plane for home and the moments leading up to the crash.

Game action, shot at DeKalb (Ga.) Memorial Stadium, consisted of two plays. After a pass fell incomplete on the final play, Herd players and coaches made the long walk back to the locker room while East Carolina players, coaches and fans whooped it up on the field.

In the locker room scene, coach Rick Tolley (played by Robert Patrick) addressed his players in a stern way. He told the players they would be home by 8 that night and they could do what they normally do on Saturday.

"When you come back Monday, your. ... is mine," Bankston said, repeating Tolley's closing lines.

Filming of the Marshall travel party getting on the jet was shot at Charlie Brown Airport in Atlanta. On the plane, Bankston said his character was seated next to the actor playing Tolley. A warehouse featuring a simulated cabin was the site for plane going down.

In the plane scene, Bankston said the passengers hear a thump as the cameras start to shake, they look at each other, then after the 3-2-1 countdown, they are told to fall forward as they look at each other again. The real plane slammed into a hillside short of the runway.

"Being on that flight now is emotional," Bankston said. "I get to see what they went through. I believe I handled it real well."

Bankston, who's retired from teaching but will return to coaching football this fall, secured his part in the film by responding to a casting call in Atlanta.

During the filming in Atlanta, Bankston and his wife, Joy, have been virtual regulars at shoots. The Bankston family came to Huntington in April to be part of the Memorial Fountain scene.

Since April 3 when filming started, Bankston has made many new friends and became reacquainted with friends, Marshall alumni and former Herd players he hadn't seen in some time. That happened June 10 when the final scene of the movie— Reggie Oliver's TD pass to Terry Gardner against Xavier and subsequent storming of the field by Marshall fans—was shot at Morris Brown College's Herndon Stadium.

"What a great story and it's been an honor and blessing to help tell it," Bankston said.

Angie McCloskey, second from left, joins her son Michael Patrick, and husband Mike, right, in looking at a 1970 Marshall team photo held by former Marshall freshman coach Mike Bankston on Saturday, June 10, 2006, during a tailgating party near the Georgia Dome prior to the filming of "We Are Marshall" at Herndon Stadium at Morris Brown College in Atlanta. Angie's father, Dave Griffith, perished in 1970 when a plane carrying 75 people crashed while returning from East Carolina University. Angie never met her father as her mother was seven months pregnant at the time of the crash.

HUNTINGTON BUSINESSMAN OPTED OUT OF FATAL FLIGHT

By David Walsh The Herald-Dispatch

HUNTINGTON—In 1970, Huntington businessman George Lambros was a regular at Cincinnati Bengals, University of Kentucky and Marshall University football games.

The owner of Lambros & Sons clothing store in downtown Huntington had a chance to travel to Greenville, N.C., on Nov. 14 to watch the Marshall Thundering Herd game against at East Carolina, but passed on the gesture by Dr. Ray Hagley and stayed home.

"Dr. Hagley begged me. It was the first jet flight. I had to beg off. Someone had to stay home and work (on Saturday) at the store," Lambros said.

That night the Lambros family was at home on High Drive. After dinner, family members gathered in front of the television. They were stunned when a bulletin flashed on the screen informing viewers about a plane being down at Tri-State Airport in Kenova. After a series of bulletins, the final word came down. The chartered jet bringing the Thundering Herd back from that 17-14 loss to the Pirates crashed short of the runway and all 75 people aboard were killed.

"I'm thinking I was supposed to be on that plane," said Lambros, 75, and now president of the Marshall M Club. "It was just awful. Think about all the families on board that plane. I spent a whole week going to funerals."

Lambros actually had to close his store one day the next week. "Everyone was in shock," he said. "You go to funerals and see moms, dads and wives. It was heart-wrenching. You never get over it."

After the crash, there was talk of Marshall eliminating its football program.

"I'm glad they didn't (drop football)," Lambros said. "We supported them all along. We never gave up hope. We believed one of these days we'd have something."

From 1971 through 1983, the Herd experienced losing season after losing season. Then came 1984 when Marshall beat East Tennessee State, 31-28, to finish 6-5. That started a run of success in the Southern Conference and then the Mid-American Conference. Today, Marshall plays in Conference USA.

"Disheartened? Yes," Lambros said in recalling sitting through those down times. "We hung in there and believed things would change. We needed resources and got them. For what we have, it's like a fairy tale come true.

"I'm real proud of the way the program has come back."

Never Forgotten

VICTIMS OF THE 1970 MARSHALL UNIVERSITY PLAN CRASH

CAPT. FRANK ABBOTT
PILOT

The Atlanta-area resident, 47, began his career with Southern Airways on July 21, 1949. He had accumulated more than 18,500 hours of total flying time, including 2,194 hours in the DC-9.

JIM ADAMS
TEAM MEMBER

A 5-foot-10, 201-pound senior offensive lineman from Mansfield, Ohio. His nickname was "Jimo." He was the son of Mr. and Mrs. Hysen Selman.

MARK ANDREWS
TEAM MEMBER

Offensive lineman. A 5-foot-11, 219-pound junior from Cincinnati. He was the son of Mr. and Mrs. Raeburn Andrews.

CHARLES "RED" ARNOLD
INSURANCE EXECUTIVE

Born in Louisville, Ky., Arnold, 42, was the general agent for Mutual of Omaha Insurance Co.

RACHEL ARNOLD
WIFE OF CHARLES ARNOLD

Rachel Arnold, 47, was born in Calhoun, Ky., and was a graduate of the Davis County Hospital School of Nursing in Owensboro, Ky. She served as a second lieutenant in the Army Nurse Corps. She and her husband were survived by four daughters.

MIKE BLAKE
TEAM MEMBER

Huntington East High School graduate. A 5-foot-11, 218-pound sophomore offensive lineman. His parents were Mr. and Mrs. Harry Goheen Jr.

DENNIS BLEVINS
TEAM MEMBER

A 6-foot, 181-pound junior wide receiver from Bluefield, W.Va. His nickname was "The Menace." He was the son of Mr. and Mrs. Solomon Blevins.

WILLIE BLUFORD
TEAM MEMBER

Linebacker from Greenwood, S.C. A 5-foot-9, 190-pound junior. He was the son of Mr. and Mrs. Willie Bluford Sr.

DONALD BOOTH
GAME FILM

Donald Booth, 42, filmed Marshall football on a volunteer basis. He was an IBM data processor for H.K. Porter Co. for 13 years. He attended Marshall and was a member of the Big Green. He was a Marine Corps vet in World War II.

DEKE BRACKETT
ASSISTANT COACH

Deke Brackett served as the Marshall kicking coach and freshman coordinator. He was a quarterback at the University of Tennessee (1931-33).

LARRY BROWN
TEAM MEMBER

Defensive lineman nicknamed "The Governor" from Atlanta, Ga. A 5-foot-9, 210-pound senior. Grandson of Mrs. Rosella Brown.

TOM BROWN
TEAM MEMBER

A 5-foot-10, 230-pound senior defensive lineman from Richmond, Va. One of several Marshall transfers from Ferrum Junior College. His parents were Mr. and Mrs. Bernard C. Brown.

AL CARELLI JR.
ASSISTANT COACH

An offensive line coach who joined the staff in February 1970. He was a graduate of Lenoir-Rhyne College in Hickory, N.C.

DR. JOSEPH CHAMBERS
TEAM PHYSICIAN

Dr. Joseph Chambers was born June 17, 1926, in Beckley. He graduated from Staunton Military Academy. He attended Duke, Marshall and Jefferson Medical College in Philadelphia. He was a member of the American, West Virginia and Cabell County medical societies.

PEGGY CHAMBERS
WIFE OF DR. JOSEPH CHAMBERS

Peggy Chambers was born Dec. 13, 1926, in Stickney, W.Va. She graduated from Charleston High School and Julliard School of Music at New York City. She was a member of Highlawn Presbyterian and Cabell County Medical Auxiliary.

ROGER CHILDERS
TEAM MEMBER

A 5-foot-10, 184-pound defensive standout from St. Albans, W.Va. He was the son of Mr. and Mrs. Donald R. Childers.

STUART COTTRELL
TEAM MEMBER

Defensive back from Eustis, Fla. A 5-foot-11, 162-pound sophomore. He was the son of Mr. and Mrs. J.D. Cottrell Jr.

RICK DARDINGER
TEAM MEMBER

Senior center from Mount Vernon, Ohio, at 5-foot-11, 215 pounds. Student body representative on the Marshall Athletic Committee. Husband of Mrs. Richard L. Dardinger.

DAVID DEBORD
TEAM MEMBER

Offensive tackle from Quincy, Fla. The 6-foot-1, 218-pound senior transferred to Marshall from Marion Institute Junior College in Alabama. He was the son of Mr. and Mrs. Frank DeBord Jr.

DANNY DEESE
CHARTER COORDINATOR

The 26-year-old Atlanta resident began his career with Southern Airways in 1964.

GARY GEORGE
SPORTS INFORMATION STUDENT ASSISTANT

Gary George, a native of Beckley, was an assistant in the sports information office. He was 20 at the time of the crash. He graduated from Woodrow Wilson High School in 1968 and served as manager of the basketball team for three years. He was a junior at Marshall and had been a reporter for The Parthenon, the school's student newspaper. He was a former employee of radio stations WJLS and WWNR in Beckley.

KEVIN GILMORE
TEAM MEMBER

A 6-foot, 187-pound halfback from Harrison, N.J. His mother was
Mrs. Marie Gilmore.

DAVE GRIFFITH
TEAM MEMBER

Dave "Griff" Griffith was a 5-foot-10, 208-pound senior defensive end from
Clarksville, Va. He played for a national championship team at Ferrum Junior
College in 1968.

DR. RAY HAGLEY
TEAM PHYSICIAN

The Huntington physician, 34, was a former president of the Marshall Alumni
Association. He was born Nov. 17, 1935. He graduated from Huntington High and
Marshall and got his medical degree at George Washington.

SHIRLEY HAGLEY
WIFE OF DR. RAY HAGLEY

Shirley Hagley was born Nov. 8, 1935. She graduated from Huntington High
School. The Hagleys had four daughters, Deborah Lynn, Karen Sue, Denice Ann and
Kimberly Leigh, and two sons, David Ray and Douglas Russell.

ART HARRIS
TEAM MEMBER

A 5-foot-10, 194-pound sophomore fullback from Passaic, N.J. A highly
recruited high school player. His father, Arthur Harris Sr., also died in the crash.

ARTHUR LAWRENCE HARRIS
FATHER OF PLAYER ART HARRIS

The 53-year-old Passaic, N.J., resident was employed with Pechter's Bakery in
Passaic. He was born in Montgomery, Ala.

BOB HARRIS
TEAM MEMBER

Backup quarterback from Cincinnati. A 5-foot-11, 181-pound junior. He was the son of Mr. and Mrs. Robert A. Harris.

E.O. HEATH
BUSINESS EXECUTIVE

Emmett O. Heath Jr., 42, was born in Oak Hill, W.Va., and had been a Huntington resident since 1960. He was a sales representative of Jantzen Sport Clothing Co., secretary and treasurer of the Midas Muffler Co. of Huntington and a U.S. Army veteran.

ELAINE HEATH
WIFE OF E.O. HEATH

Elaine Heath, 42, was born in Pittsburgh and graduated from the nursing school at the University of Pennsylvania. She was president of the Midas Muffler Co. of Huntington. She and her husband were survived by two sons and two daughters.

BOBBY JOE HILL
TEAM MEMBER

Versatile player at defensive back and wide receiver. A 5-foot-10, 163-pound sophomore from Dallas, Texas. His parents were Mr. and Mrs. Aaron Hill Sr.

JOE HOOD
TEAM MEMBER

A 6-foot-1, 197-pound sophomore halfback. He was a prep star at Druid High School in Tuscaloosa, Ala. He was the son of Mr. and Mrs. James Brown.

TOM HOWARD
TEAM MEMBER

Offensive lineman and punter from Milton. A 5-foot-10, 212-pound junior. He was the son of Mr. and Mrs. James Howard.

JAMES JARRELL
SUPPORTER

James Jarrell, 37, was manager of the Guyan Lumber Co. Born in Hamlin, W.Va., he was a graduate of the Kentucky Military Institute and Indiana University and served as an intelligence officer in the U.S. Army.

CYNTHIA JARRELL
WIFE OF JAMES JARRELL

Cynthia Jarrell, 34, was born in Indianapolis and attended Indiana University. She was a member of several organizations, including the Huntington Woman's Club.

KEN JONES
WHTN-TV 13 SPORTS DIRECTOR

Ken Jones, 43, served as sports director at WHTN-TV in Huntington. He was born May 30, 1927, in Indianapolis. He was a member of the West Virginia Sportscasters Association and was named Sportscaster of the Year in 1969. He was a member at Spring Valley Country Club. He was survived by his wife, Lois Anderson Jones, and three sons, Kristopher, Jeffrey and Phillip.

CHARLIE KAUTZ
ATHLETIC DIRECTOR

Charlie Kautz went from acting athletic director to permanent AD on Nov. 20, 1969. He was Huntington native and was married to Lucy Gawthrop. He graduated from Huntington High School in 1943. He received his bachelor's from Marshall in 1949 and his master's, also at Marshall, in 1952. He served as an assistant or head coach of all sports at Marshall at one time or another, with the exception of golf, tennis and wrestling. He compiled a 74-25-1 mark as head football coach at Ceredo-Kenova, Ironton and Rock Hill high schools before joining the Marshall staff in 1961. He was member of the Marine Corps. during World War II and Korean War.

MARCELLO LAJTERMAN
TEAM MEMBER

Kicker from Lyndhurst. N.J. A 6-foot, 178-pound sophomore who was a high school teammate of quarterback Ted Shoebridge. His parents were Mr. and Mrs. Israel Lajterman.

RICK LECH
TEAM MEMBER

Rick Lech was a 5-foot-9, 169-pound junior defensive back from Columbus, Ohio. He also played on the Marshall baseball team. He was the son of Mr. and Mrs. Richard A. Lech.

FRANK LORIA
ASSISTANT COACH

Defensive backs coach from Clarksburg, W.Va. He was a two-time All-American safety at Virginia Tech (1966-67) and a College Football Hall of Fame inductee (1999).

GENE MOREHOUSE
SPORTS INFORMATION DIRECTOR AND RADIO ANNOUNCER

Gene Morehouse, "The Voice of the Herd," came to Marshall in July 1968 after a 22-year career in broadcasting. He was one of the few sports information directors who handled radio play-by-play for football and basketball. Morehouse, a native of Newark, N.J., came to West Virginia in 1949 and called Beckley his "hometown." He served as general manager of WFEA in Manchester, N.H., and WJLS in Beckley and doubled as a sports announcer. He was voted West Virginia's outstanding sportscaster in 1963 and 1965. He was Air Force veteran and holder of a Bronze Star Medal.

JIM "SHORTY" MOSS
ASSISTANT COACH

Marshall offensive coordinator. He graduated Huntington East High School graduate in 1958. He was a West Virginia University team captain in 1962. He was drafted by the New York Giants and Oakland Raiders.

BARRY NASH
TEAM MEMBER

Sophomore from Man, W.Va. The bodies of Barry Nash, Kevin Gilmore, Allen Skeens, Tom Zborill, Dave Griffith and Tom Brown couldn't be identified, and they were buried in adjacent graves next to a monument in Spring Hill Cemetery overlooking the Marshall football stadium. He was the son of the late Rev. Normal A. Nash and Weltha Frye Nash and the brother of Doris Adkins, Normal A. Nash Jr., Brenda Sparks, Sandra Merritt, Sheila Nash-Foster, Stephen Nash, Mary Hope Wallace, Donna Flowers, Martha Ferguson, Susan Sperry, Sherry Flesher, Bill Nash and the late Paul Hunter Nash.

JEFF NATHAN
REPORTER FOR THE PARTHENON STUDENT NEWSPAPER

Jeff Nathan, a junior from Parkersburg, W.Va., served as sports editor of The Parthenon, Marshall's student newspaper.

PAT NORRELL
TEAM MEMBER

Offensive lineman known as "Nutsy." a 5-foot-11, 192-pound senior from Hartsdale, N.Y. He was the son of Mr. and Mrs R.H. Norrell.

DR. BRIAN O'CONNOR
DIRECTOR OF ADMISSIONS

Dr. Brian O'Connor, 32, was director of admissions at Marshall. He had joined the Marshall staff 18 months prior to the crash. He was born Sept. 1, 1938, in Staten Island, N.Y. He got his bachelor's from Wagner, master's from Indiana and Ph.D. from Denver University.

BOB PATTERSON
TEAM MEMBER

Patterson was a 6-foot-2, 215-pound offensive lineman from Lewisburg, N.C. He played two seasons at Ferrum Junior College. He was the son of Mrs. Marvin Pleasants.

CHARLENE POAT
FLIGHT ATTENDANT FOR SOUTHERN AIRWAYS

Charlene Poat, a 28-year-old College Park, Ga., resident, was a native of Paducah, Ky. She had completed her last recurrent flight training on Oct. 22, 1970.

MICHAEL PRESTERA
FORMER BIG GREEN PRESIDENT AND DELEGATE-ELECT TO THE WEST VIRGINIA LEGISLATURE

Michael Prestera, 60, was president of C.L. Whitten Transfer Co., and Prestera Trucking Company. He was born Nov. 18, 1909, in Bradford. He got his certificate of pharmacy at Pennsylvania. He received chemistry and personnel management degrees from Alabama. He was a former Big Green Club president and delegate-elect to the West Virginia Legislature. He was former president of the Tri-State Area Council, Boy Scouts of America.

DR. GLENN PRESTON
TEAM DENTIST

Preston, 47, was an oral surgeon. He was born June 12, 1923, in Lawrence Co., Ky. He graduated from Huntington High, Marshall and Northwestern University Dental School. He was an Army veteran of World War II.

PHYLLIS PRESTON
WIFE OF DR. GLENN PRESTON

Phyllis Preston was born July 29, 1925, in Huntington. She attended Huntington High School and Wiseman School of Business. She and her husband left behind three daughters, Mrs. Carolle Wright (of Knoxville), Mrs. Kimberly Lewis and Beverly Preston.

DR. H.D. PROCTOR
TEAM PHYSICIAN

He was born July 30, 1927, in Landisburg, W.Va. He graduated from Marshall and Emory School of Medicine in Atlanta. He was a member of the Big Green Club and Masonic Order. He was a Navy veteran and served in World War II.

COURTNEY PROCTOR
WIFE OF DR. H.D. PROCTOR

Courtney Proctor was born Oct. 11, 1928, in Fayetteville, W.Va. She graduated from Fayetteville High School.

MURRILL RALSTEN
HUNTINGTON CITY COUNCILMAN

Murrill Ralsten, 38, operated Ralsten Ltd., a clothing store at 1531 4th Ave. in Huntington

HELEN RALSTEN
WIFE OF MURRILL RALSTEN

Helen Ralsten, 32, was born in Weirton, W.Va., and was a former schoolteacher. She and her husband were survived by a son and a daughter.

SCOTTIE REESE
TEAM MEMBER

Played defensive end and linebacker. A 5-foot-11, 182-pound junior from Waco, Texas. He was the son of Mr. and Mrs. Chester Reese.

JACK REPASY
TEAM MEMBER

Jack Repasy was a sure-handed wide receiver from Cincinnati. A 6-foot, 172-pound junior. He was the son of Mr. and Mrs. John A. Repasy.

LARRY SANDERS
TEAM MEMBER

Was considered a pro prospect in the defensive secondary. A 6-foot-3, 193-pound junior from Tuscaloosa, Ala. He was the son of Mr. and Mrs. Lucian Sanders Jr.

AL SAYLOR
TEAM MEMBER

A 5-foot-10, 200-pound sophomore defensive end from Cuyahoga Falls, Ohio. His parents were Mr. and Mrs. Bruce Saylor.

JIM SCHROER
HEAD ATHLETIC TRAINER

Jim Schroer, 28 and a Cincinnati native, joined the Marshall staff in January 1970. He came from Toledo, where he had served as athletic trainer and physical education instructor since 1968. He received his bachelor's degree from Cincinnati in 1964 and did his graduate work at Toledo in 1965-66.

ART SHANNON
TEAM MEMBER

A 5-foot-9, 200-pound junior linebacker from Greensboro, N.C. Shannon was a transfer from Ferrum Junior College. He was the son of Mr. and Mrs. L.G. Shannon.

TED SHOEBRIDGE
TEAM MEMBER

Marshall's starting quarterback known as "Shoe" was a 5-foot-10, 195-pound junior from Lyndhurst, N.J., He was the son of Mr. and Mrs. L.T. Shoebridge.

ALLEN SKEENS
TEAM MEMBER

Sophomore from Ravenswood, W.Va. One of the six players whose bodies couldn't be positively identified, he is buried next to a monument in Spring Hill Cemetery. He was the son of Mr. and Mrs. D.E. Skeens.

JERRY SMITH
FIRST OFFICER FOR SOUTHERN AIRWAYS

Jerry Smith began his career with Southern Airways on April 12, 1965. The 28-year-old Stone Mountain, Ga., resident had accumulated more than 5,800 hours of total flying time, including 1,196 hours in the DC-9.

JERRY STAINBACK
TEAM MEMBER

A junior college All-American linebacker who came to Marshall from Ferrum Junior College. A 5-foot-10, 199-pound senior from Newport News, Va. He was the husband of Mrs. Jerry Stainback Jr.

DONALD TACKETT
STUDENT TRAINER

Donald Tackett, 23, was an assistant football trainer. He was born March 2, 1947, in Logan. His home was Dingess. He graduated from Lenore High in 1966 and enrolled at Marshall later that year. He was a member of the National Athletic Trainers Association.

RICK TOLLEY
HEAD COACH

Rick Tolley became head coach in 1970 after serving as the interim head coach in 1969. He joined the staff as an assistant coach in 1969. He was a graduate of VPI and Mullens (W.Va.) High School.

ROBERT VANHORN
TEAM MEMBER

One of several Marshall players from Druid High School in Tuscaloosa, Ala. A 6-foot-1, 210-pound sophomore defensive tackle. He was the son of Mr. and Mrs. Elijah VanHorn.

ROGER VANOVER
TEAM MEMBER

A 6-foot-2, 204-pound junior tight end from Russell, Ky. He also played Marshall freshman basketball in the 1968-69 season. His parents were Mr. and Mrs. Phillip R. Pruitt.

PATRICIA VAUGHT
FLIGHT ATTENDANT FOR SOUTHERN AIRWAYS

Patricia Vaught began her career with Southern Airways on June 11, 1962. The 27-year-old East Point, Ga., resident completed her last recurrent flight training on Oct. 21, 1970.

PARKER WARD
AUTOMOBILE DEALER

Born in Cincinnati, Parker Ward, 36, was vice president and general manager of Hez Ward Buick. He was a graduate of the University of North Carolina and General Motors Institute. He was survived by two sons and two daughters.

NORMAN WEICHMANN
TEAM MEMBER

Norman Weichmann, who lived in South Point, Ohio, filmed Marshall football games with Donald Booth. They did it as volunteers, since the school didn't have an official photographer. He was manager of Pigments Division/Chemetron Corp. in Huntington. He was responsible for five plants, one of which was in Canada. He was survived by his wife, Jane Wagner, and two daughters, Cynthia and Katherine.

FREDDY WILSON
TEAM MEMBER

Starting tight end as a 6-foot-3, 222-pound sophomore. Another product of Druid High School in Tuscaloosa, Ala. His father was Mr. Wilbert Wilson.

JOHN YOUNG
TEAM MEMBER

A 6-foot-3, 192-pound sophomore end from Buckhannon, W.Va. High school teammate of Marshall defensive tackle Fred Gaudet. He was the son of Mr. and Mrs. F.P. Young.

TOM ZBORILL
TEAM MEMBER

Junior defensive lineman from Richmond, Va. A 6-foot, 210-pound transfer from Ferrum Junior College. His father was Walter F. Zborill Jr.

DAUGHTER REMEMBERS HER PARENTS

(Editor's note: Cindy Arnold Pierce's parents, Charles Arnold and Rachel Baker Arnold, were among the 75 people killed in the Marshall plane crash Nov. 14, 1970. Her parents relocated their family to Huntington one year earlier in order for her father to run the office of Mutual of Omaha. He was the general agent. Her mother was a nurse.)

As Nov. 14 approaches, my mind ultimately flickers back to that night in 1970, 33 years ago. I was 12 years old and living in Huntington with my parents and sisters. I had a great life. I thought my father was the funniest man alive and was sure there was no one more attractive than my mother. I was making the transition from elementary school to junior high. I loved making friends of all the "new" kids from other schools and changing classes every period. Going to school mixes was the best! What a great and exciting time. I felt I was growing up and moving into the big world.

We had only lived in Huntington for a little over a year. So, my parents were very excited to be asked to accompany the Marshall University football team at an away game against East Carolina.

They joined the Marshall football team players, coaches and other supporters on the chartered plane. Alas, Marshall lost that Saturday, but I knew my parents would be home that evening. I was excited to talk to them about the players they may have met.

That evening it was raining, but I don't remember ever registering any concern. As the evening got later, I began wondering what was delaying my parents' return. The TV news announced a plane had crashed at the Tri-State Airport, but the report was that is was a private plane.

My sister kept trying to call the airport, and they told her the same thing, "No, it was a private plane."

Then, finally, the TV announcement was made. Yes, there was a plane crash, and yes it was the Marshall University chartered plane.

Thinking with a child's mind, I just could not believe this was true. Like a movie with a twist, I kept waiting for my parents to come home to hold and comfort me for the scare I had experienced.

However, the time kept ticking, and people kept showing up at our house, but not my parents. On the news they said they were looking for survivors. I went from

Cindy Arnold Pierce's parents were killed in the November 14, 1970, Marshall plane crash.

Cindy Arnold around the time of the Marshall University plane crash, which claimed the lives of her parents.

not believing to hoping and praying someone would find them alive.

As more time went by and more hope was gone, I prayed to God to bring one back. I would not tell him which one, just please, please bring one.

Our house filled up. One of my younger sister's friends took her to their house. Then one of my friend's parents took me. They put me to bed, and I remember telling them to wake me up if there was any news. They never awakened me. The next morning, I learned all 75 people on board had been killed.

This was devastating to each family that lost someone, but it did not stop there. The whole town was devastated. The young men all had parents, sisters, brothers, friends and fans. Then there were the adults on board who left spouses, children, siblings, parents, co-workers and friends.

The town was in shock, and the country grieved with us.

I remember hearing people talking about us. They said, "Those poor children", "What are they going to do?" and "She just does not understand."

I remember thinking, "I can hear you," and "I do so understand." What I knew was that I had lost the two most important people in my life.

What I did not really know and what those people meant was how this loss would affect my future. My support system and most important role models were lost as I grew and encountered life's challenges. Beyond my immediate loss, I was not considering graduation, relationship advice, educational decisions and just the everyday closeness and emotional support only loving parents provide.

After all the funerals and memorial services where completed, real life set in. We had to adjust to being without our parents, and it was a greater hardship because of the short time we had lived in Huntington. We did not have the neighbors and friends we had known all of our lives. No one knew our names. We were "The girls that lost their parents."

We found that people are people, and you must take the good with the bad. There were those who focused on everything we did and enjoyed spreading rumors and gossip. And, unfortunately, there were people who were interested in us only because my parents had left some inheritance. Through this experience, I observed that money can corrupt even the most well-intentioned people. Many others were caring, good-hearted people truly concerned with our situation. And then there was our grandmother, who loved us unconditionally.

So, what am I like now? Today, I consider myself a happy person, just like when I was 12. I have a wonderful husband and his family, great old friends and new, and I still have my loving sisters.

I chose not to have children, the time was never right. Maybe I feared the possibility of leaving them. My youngest sister has four children, however, allowing us all the opportunity to share them.

I have a successful career which makes me wonder if I approach work like my mom or dad. Once, my uncle described how my parents would tackle a situation or problem. He said my father would chop the top off of mountains to quickly reach a solution while my mother would go down in each valley to investigate and thoroughly understand all aspects of a situation. I am like my mom!

Recently, my sister went through my grandmother's belongings and found a letter from my mother. It was, most likely, the last letter mom ever wrote to her. Mom's letter describes what was going on in each of her children's lives and was filled with humorous comments and interesting details. In one section, she spoke of losing a pet. As my husband read my mother's sad comments about our pet, he looked at me and said, "Who does that sound like?" He could not have said anything to make me feel more proud.

Not only do I continually wonder how my parents and I were alike, but I also wish I knew what they thought of me as a child. Was I a handful? Did they think I was funny, smart or clever?

For this and many other reasons, I would like to advise everyone to love your family, each day as if it were the last day you would see them. Take time to record the little details and interesting occurrences in your family's life. Ask your children questions such as what do they like about themselves, what is their favorite thing to do with mom and what is funny about dad. Hopefully, they will always have someone to tell them those interesting stories from the past, but whatever the situation, they will always appreciate you for spending the time to preserve memories they can read over and over again.

To Charles Arnold and Rachel Baker Arnold, I would like to say thank you for our short time together. Huntington may not have had the time to know you well, but I did. I only have to look in the mirror to see familiar eyes and hair. I know you are looking down on all of us and are very proud. Also, I guess you have noticed, Marshall's football team has improved! One last thing, someday when I join you up there, be prepared to sit down and spend quite some time telling me more and more of our family history and stories.

Cindy Arnold Pierce lives in Freeland, Mich.

IN HIS FATHER'S FOOTSTEPS

DECADES AFTER CRASH, MOREHOUSE FINISHING JOB

By Mark Truby, The Herald-Dispatch

Gene Morehouse was the radio voice of the Herd from 1968 until he died in the Marshall University plane crash on November. 14, 1970.

Nine-year-old Keith Morehouse didn't know his future was charted when his father died in the Marshall University plane crash 27 years ago today.

All he knew was his dad, Gene Morehouse, was a neat guy who brightened the house when he came home at night. And he had the coolest job around as play-by-play radio broadcaster for Marshall football and basketball games. He was the voice of Marshall sports.

And then he was gone, killed along with 74 others when a DC-9 carrying the 1970 Marshall football team, boosters and flight crew crashed near Tri-State Airport the evening of Nov. 14, 1970.

One of six children, Morehouse grew up fatherless in the shadow of the crash, still the worst tragedy in U.S. sports history. Twenty-nine children lost parents on Southern Airways Flight 932. They became Huntington's daughters and sons as a wounded community looked after its own following the crash.

It was the connection between those who lost loved ones that day that drew Morehouse to Debbie Hagley, whose mother and father died in the crash. She would become his wife.

Morehouse signed up for broadcast journalism classes at Marshall. And after 13 years as a TV news and sports reporter, Marshall called one day.

Would he become the voice of Marshall sports?

A voice that had been speaking to him softly for years became louder and clearer. He thought of his father, his family and Huntington.

"I felt like it was time to finish the job," Morehouse says.

RADIO DAYS

Gene Morehouse was raised in Newark, N.J., and graduated from high school in New York City. He went to Columbia University from 1940 to 1942, leaving at 20 to join the Army Air Corps and fight in World War II. He earned the Bronze Star for courage in combat.

In 1946, while a reporter for the New York Daily Fruit Reporter, he married New Yorker Genevieve Vivlamore.

Gene Morehouse was a broadcaster to the bone and that passion carried him and Gen to small towns such as Keokuk, Iowa, before they landed in West Virginia.

In 1949, he became sports and news director at WWNR in Beckley. Save for a two-year stint in Manchester, N.H., the Morehouses lived in Beckley until 1967.

During that time he averaged more than 50 play-by-play broadcasts a year, calling high school sports and semiprofessional football.

Perhaps more than anything, Gene Morehouse was known for his 16 years as the voice of Beckley's Flying Eagles. In 1959 and 1960, he called football games played by a Beckley football star named Bobby Pruett.

"I remember Keith's dad very vividly," says Pruett, now Marshall's head football coach. "He was a great guy and an outstanding announcer."

His peers recognized his professionalism by naming him West Virginia's outstanding sportscaster in 1963 and 1965.

In July 1968, Gene, then 46, reluctantly moved his family from Beckley to become Marshall's sports information director and radio play-by-play announcer.

"He had to have both jobs, that's the only way he would do it because he had six children to support," Keith Morehouse says.

Far from the winning ways of Beckley's Woodrow Wilson High School, Marshall was coming off a dismal 0-10 season in 1967. During Gene Morehouse's first year behind the microphone, the team didn't fare much better at 0-9-1.

Their futility was the subject of jokes, their athletic facilities the laughingstock of the Mid-American Conference. In 1969, in the face of 144 alleged recruiting violations, Marshall was booted from the MAC.

Even during these depressing days for Marshall football, Gene Morehouse gained the respect of his staff.

"He was a very kind individual and an easy person to work with and for," says Joe Wortham, Marshall's concessions manager, who worked for Gene Morehouse keeping stats for Marshall games. "He was really doing two full-time jobs and worked hard at both. He took pride in his radio work. It wasn't something he did lightly. He would spend many hours memorizing names and facts."

He also earned the respect of the sports writers covering the Herd, who typically eyed broadcasters warily.

"He was a newsperson as much as he was a broadcaster," says Ernie Salvatore, columnist and former sports editor for The Herald-Dispatch. "That's why he always got along with the sports reporters. He was like me, an Easterner who fell in love with West Virginia and stayed."

In 1969, under new football coach Rick Tolley, the disgraced Marshall football team snapped a 27-game winless streak with a homecoming win over Bowling Green. The team won three games that year.

"When Dad was with Marshall they were struggling and on probation," says Keith's older brother, Steve Morehouse. "But Dad was smart enough to know they had a bright future."

In 1970, the Herd managed another three wins and nearly pulled off a victory on Nov. 14 against East Carolina at Greenville, N.C. That chilly afternoon, 37 team members, five coaches, 21 boosters, seven university employees and a five-member flight crew loaded onto the team plane and winged back toward Huntington. Gene Morehouse was on the plane. So were Debbie Hagley's parents, Ray and Shirley Hagley.

On the approach to Tri-State Airport, a faulty altimeter deceived the pilots into thinking they were 400 feet higher than they actually were. The plane slammed into a hillside west of the airport, tore a 95-foot gash in the earth and broke apart in flames on the foggy, rainy night.

There were no survivors.

'A NATURAL FIT'

Keith Morehouse isn't sure exactly when it clicked that he wanted to be a sports announcer. The seed may have been planted when he played on the court after Herd basketball games while his father wrapped up a broadcast.

In the next few years, while his mother, a registered nurse at Cabell Huntington Hospital, worked and raised six children, Keith's love for sports began to have a purpose.

"I can remember being in the eighth grade thinking that I might want to go into sports broadcasting," he says.

His brothers and sisters remember his dream more clearly.

"Keith seemed to always have in mind what he wanted to do for a career, while the rest of us were normal people and couldn't figure out what we wanted," Steve Morehouse says.

"I remember that it seemed like a natural fit because he was always so outgoing and was so interested in sports," says Gail McDowell, Keith's oldest sibling.

After high school, he enrolled in broadcast journalism classes, learning the craft from former WSAZ anchorman Bos Johnson. Fresh from college, Morehouse took a job as a part-time news reporter with WOWK-TV.

"For a while, I did news almost exclusively, all the while knowing I wanted to eventually get into sports," he recalls.

Long hours, modest pay and nerve-jangling deadlines are the life of a young reporter, but Keith Morehouse had no regrets.

"I enjoy the exhilaration of live television," he says. "It's live and you can't go back and do it over again."

Within a few years he was occasionally covering sports and then, finally, he was promoted to weekend sports anchor.

In late 1995, when WOWK's lead sports anchor, Dave Maetzold, left Huntington for a job in Columbus, Ohio, Morehouse hoped he would be picked for the top job.

Keith Morehouse met his future wife, Debbie, in Myrtle Beach after graduating from Huntington High School in 1979. Morehouse, who lost his father, Gene, in the Marshall plane crash, found he had a special bond with Debbie, whose parents, Ray and Shirley Hagley, also died in the crash.

"I asked for the job, I thought I deserved it, but they decided they wanted to go in another direction," Morehouse says. WOWK hired Dave Furst, who has since left Huntington to work in a bigger market.

For the first time, Keith Morehouse seriously considered leaving Huntington.

'AN INDELIBLE BOND'

Senior week in Myrtle Beach, S.C., is a Mountain State rite of passage.

Diplomas and graduation cash in hand, new high school graduates head to the coast for seven days of unreserved fun before the summer jobs begin.

In 1979, Keith Morehouse and Debbie Hagley met at a beach bar called Castaways. Debbie graduated from Huntington East, Keith went to Huntington High. They had never met.

A few minutes into their first conversation, the two teen-agers found they had more in common than the Class of '79.

"It came up pretty soon after we met each other," says Debbie Morehouse, who is also one of six children. "Keith asked me if my parents were in the crash. I told him they were. And that was pretty much it."

Without having had a single conversation they had shared experiences that would shape the rest of their lives.

"I had never met her but I recognized her name," Morehouse says. "I had seen the names of people associated with the crash so many times it was burned into my brain."

Before long they were dating. Six years later they were married.

"Would we have gotten together if our parents weren't in the plane crash?" Keith Morehouse says, repeating the question as he considers it. "I don't know. We understand things about each other that I'm not sure anyone else could."

Cozy is the word the mind conjures when you visit the Morehouses' home on brick-surfaced, tree-lined 15th Street. They live in a comfortable two-story home with their son, Lake, 6, a blond-haired first-grader who forever has a question on his lips.

A small picture frame in their living room holds a card that reads: "A small town is like a big family."

It's more than a Hallmark phrase to the Morehouses. After the crash, the community did its best to fill the void created in their lives.

"The crash formed a deep and indelible bond with the people who live in the city," Morehouse says. "I understand that some people may not want to hear about it anymore. But for us and other people involved it's always going to be a big part of our lives. I mean, our son doesn't have any grandparents now that my mom died a few years ago."

Twenty-seven years have eased the pain of the memories. Marshall's success in academics and athletics has been a fitting tribute to the crash victims. A modern football field has replaced rickety Fairfield Stadium and new academic buildings have popped up all over campus.

"Most of it is positive now," Morehouse says. "I truly think it's a unique story. We have seen the abyss. No school in the country has gone through what Marshall has."

IN HIS FATHER'S FOOTSTEPS

In 1996, Morehouse moved to rival station WSAZ, to work as a sportscaster and the play-by-play announcer for Marshall football broadcasts.

"They had been talking to (former WSAZ sports anchor) Kevin Nathan, but he got another job and moved," Keith Morehouse said. "Then they called me. I was extremely flattered that my name came up."

In the separate experiences of father and son, you could find evidence of Marshall's rise from disgrace and tragedy.

Gene Morehouse announced 16 football games over two seasons before he called

Actor Matthew McConaughey, left, speaks to WSAZ sports director Keith Morehouse, right, after a news conference in April 2006. Morehouse's father, Gene Morehouse, was killed in the 1970 plane crash. McConaughey portrays the coach of the 1971 team in the movie "We Are Marshall."

a Marshall win. Keith Morehouse didn't announce a Marshall football loss until his 16th game as the TV voice of the Herd - the 1997 season opener against West Virginia University.

The father was in his second year in Huntington when Marshall was kicked out of the MAC for a laundry list of NCAA violations. In the son's second season as Marshall's play-by-play man, the Herd made a historical return to NCAA division I-A and the MAC.

"I never consciously set out to become the Marshall play-by-play guy," Morehouse said. "But I worked hard over the years and when the opportunity came, I felt I was ready. I'd like to think I have been successful because of my father and also because I have worked hard."

Keith Morehouse's sister, Gail McDowell, as well as his wife, expressed pride in his accomplishments.

"We always said it was a shame that Dad died because he would have been so proud of Keith," she said. "He worked hard to carry on where Dad left off."

In 2006, Morehouse continues in his role of sports director at WSAZ as an anchor working out of the Huntington studio. He stays close to Marshall as a reporter covering the Thundering Herd. His duties also include hosting the Marshall Magazine program and Marshall football and men's basketball coaches' shows.

WITH EACH PASSING MEMORIAL SERVICE, FAMILIES NEVER FORGET

By Michael Prestera

Amy Prestera wasn't yet born when her grandfather, Michael Prestera, was killed in the crash.

"I've heard he was wonderful, and I've heard about his efforts and his energy," she told The Herald-Dispatch in November 1997. Prestera was a member of the West Virginia House of Delegates when he died.

"People who don't know much about this, or who didn't have family in it, just don't know the significance of it," Prestera said. "It's one of the most important days of my life and the lives of those families of all the victims."

Aside from his passion for Marshall football, he was heavily involved with the university and the greater Huntington community. His 55-year-old son, Michael Prestera, who was 20 when the crash occurred, said his father was among many dedicated Huntingtonians whose lives ended too soon.

"To me, it's a celebration of who they were and how they lived," he said of the annual memorial service at the Marshall Memorial Student Center plaza. "It's remembering what they meant, not necessarily how they died. ... There is so much effect these people did have within the community."

BARRY NASH

Four sisters of Barry Nash, who was one of the 37 football players killed in the crash, attended the memorial ceremony in 1998. They were Sheila Nash Foster, Sandra Merritt, Donna Flowers and Mary Wallace.

"He's still very much alive," Foster said of her brother. "We still talk about him. Our grandchildren feel like they know him."

The pain after the crash was horrible for Nash's mother, his sisters said, because

their 18-year-old brother, Paul, had died of a heart condition nearly four years to the day before the crash.

Not only that, but Nash's body was one of six that could not be positively identified after the crash.

"Our mother screamed for a body to bury beside Paul," Wallace said.

Nash and the other five unidentified victims are buried in a common grave in Spring Hill Cemetery in Huntington.

MIKE BLAKE

Debbie Goheen of Huntington, whose brother, Mike Blake, was one of the players killed in the crash, did not attend the ceremony in 1998 because it was scheduled for the day before the anniversary of the crash.

"I wish there'd been a little more advance notice if it wasn't going to be held on the 14th," Goheen said. She said she hopes the memorial services will never stop, and will always be conducted on Nov. 14.

"Some people made some major sacrifices," Goheen said. "The healing needs to continue."

FRANK LORIA

Frank Loria Jr. was born one month after his dad, then-assistant coach Frank Loria, died in the crash. Frank Loria was 23.

"Everything I do is to honor him," Loria Jr. said of his dad.

His visit to Huntington in 2000 from his New Jersey home was his first ever.

"I always wanted to know more," he said. "It's opened a lot of feelings. I don't know if it's better. I wish I had that relationship with my father."

He watched the "Ashes to Glory" documentary Sunday with family in Clarksburg.

"We sat there in total silence," he said.

CHARLIE KAUTZ

Huntington resident Lucianne Kautz Call's father, then-Marshall athletic director Charlie Kautz, died in the crash.

Call admitted it was difficult to attend the service in 2000. But, she's glad she did.

"It was fabulous," she said.

Call still mourns her father, but has come a long way. In fact, she now is a flight attendant with U.S. Airways and flies into and out of Tri-State Airport. One of her dreams is to see a regional airport built.

Soon after word of the Marshall tragedy was spread across the nation, donations for victims' families began pouring in. Less than a month before the Marshall crash, 13 members of the Wichita State football team died in a plane crash in Silver Plume, Colorado. A national television broadcast of the stories prompted donations for both.

PARKER WARD

The silencing of the Memorial Fountain at Marshall University always helps Mary Plyde Ward Bell accept the tragedy that happened to her family and so many others in 1970.

"When the water is turned off, there's a stillness and a calmness," Bell said at the memorial service in 2003. "It's a peaceful acceptance." Bell's husband Parker Ward, a Marshall supporter, left behind his wife and four children.

The university and the community came together to support the families, especially the children, Bell said.

"Some of the players would come to the homes, and the Athletic Department would provide packets for the child with little recordings of Marshall songs," she said. "We were invited to be a part of ceremonies and functions. We were never forgotten."

Cindy, Tara and Debbie Chambers, whose parents, Dr. Joseph and Margaret Chambers were passengers on the ill-fated football team charter airliner, at the dedication of a new cheerleaders' dressing room in October 1971.

DR. H.D. "PETE" AND
COURTNEY PROCTOR

John Proctor, of Huntington, and his siblings lost their parents, Dr. H.D. "Pete" and Courtney Proctor. Proctor was 5 years old and can remember being told his parents were gone. He, too, has always felt the community's support, he said at the memorial service in 2003.

"In a way, I lost my parents, but I probably gained 80 or 90," he said. "Other kids of the crash would say the same thing."

MURRILL AND HELEN RALSTEN

John and Carol Ralsten traveled from Parkersburg to Huntington for one purpose: to celebrate family.

John Ralsten's brother, Murrill Ralsten, and his wife Helen, died 35 years ago in what has been called "the darkest night" in Marshall University's and Huntington's history. Although the memorial ceremony has taken place each year since the crash, the service in 2005 was the Ralstens' first.

"We've just come to honor them," Carol Ralsten said. "It's so nice to see that people haven't forgotten."

MEMORIAL FOUNTAIN DESIGNED TO REPRESENT 'UPWARD GROWTH, IMMORTALITY, ETERNALITY'

By Bob Withers, The Herald-Dispatch

HUNTINGTON—The graceful Memorial Fountain that stands in front of the campus entrance to Marshall University's Memorial Student Center was designed to reaffirm "purposeful life" as much as mourn "tragic loss" after the deaths of the 75 football players, coaches and fans who died in the tragic crash of Nov. 14, 1970.

"Let us move with firm resolve to take up the unfinished tasks of this great institution and find personal significance and lasting stimulus in this memorial dedication," said Lawrence Tippett, a member of the Marshall University Foundation board, when the fountain and its integral Harry Bertoia sculpture were dedicated Nov. 12, 1972.

As the waters began to rise and fall through the structure, Bertoia said he hoped they would commemorate "upward growth, immortality, eternality."

Acting Marshall President Donald Dedmon had appointed a Memorial Committee—members of which included Dr. Eugene Hoak, professor of speech; Dr. James E. Phipps, president of the Alumni Association; and Dr. Constantine W. Curris, director of student personnel programs—shortly after the crash to decide on an appropriate memorial to those who perished therein.

The committee decided that the major memorial should be located on campus, but also that two smaller remembrances should be constructed—plaques and a memory garden at Fairfield Stadium and a granite cenotaph at Spring Hill Cemetery, where the six unidentified players were buried. The student center, which also was finished about that time, was designated a memorial to the crash victims as well.

An early suggestion for the campus memorial, proposed by Park Commissioner G.Y. Neal, called for a

Workers install the 6,500-pound Memorial Fountain in October 1972.

Workers build walls around the newly installed Memorial Fountain in October 1972 so they may finish plumbing work before the fountain was officially unveiled November 12, 1972.

reinforced concrete pilaster covered with white marble and supporting a bronze statue of a football player.

But it was Bertoia, an internationally known Italian artist, who came up with a $25,000 design employing bronze, copper tubing and welding rods that pleased the committee and took a year and a half to complete.

One piece of trivia about the sculpture—that there are 75 copper tubes, one for each person lost in the tragedy—is not true. Almost 150 tubes in the work sweep toward the sky.

The 6,500-pound, 13-foot-high sculpture was trucked to Huntington on a flatbed trailer from Bertoia's home in Barto, Pa. A crane moved it into place in the middle of the fountain on Oct. 18, 1972, nearly a month before the dedication. A wooden structure surrounded it while plumbing and electrical work was completed.

Workers from the F.C. McColm Granite Co., a Huntington monument firm, installed a permanent plaque on a base supplied by Neighborgall Construction Co. in front of the fountain on Aug. 10, 1973.

The plaque, which replaced a temporary one, read as follows:

"They shall live on in the hearts of their families and friends forever and this memorial records their loss to the university and the community."

Ed McComas reads over the names on the Marshall Memorial Fountain prior to a memorial service Nov. 14, 2005, honoring the 75 people who died on Nov. 14, 1970, when the plane carrying Marshall football players, coaches, staff, supporters and flight crew crashed into a mountain near the Huntington Tri-State airport. McComas was a freshman attending Marshall at the time of the crash. He says he had class with several of the players killed. This was his first memorial service.

MARSHALL MEMORIAL BRONZE UNVEILED TO MIX OF EMOTIONS

By Dave Wellman, The Herald-Dispatch

HUNTINGTON—For a while they were so quiet, totally unlike Marshall University football fans.

They listened politely to the speeches, and then watched with anticipation as the green cover came off the "We Are Marshall Memorial Bronze."

And then, they erupted. Wild applause. Whistles. Cheers.

And tears.

"I'm speechless," Carol Palmer said Saturday, her eyes glued to the bronze. "It just fills you with such a feeling."

Thousands of Marshall fans gathered in the west parking lot of Marshall Stadium 90 minutes before the Thundering Herd whipped Miami (Ohio), 51-31, to witness the unveiling of the bronze.

The 17-by-23-foot statue, a gift to the university from Marshall fans, and the idea of John and Ann Krieger of Huntington, is a monument to the 75 people who died in the 1970 MU plane crash.

"Perfect," Ann Krieger said after the ceremony.

The huge crowd included many former Thundering Herd players and current supporters living nearby and far away.

Tony Barile, who now lives in Fairfax, Va., was a senior on the 1970 team. He missed the plane trip to East Carolina after suffering a lacerated kidney in practice two weeks earlier.

"Oh, it's wonderful," Barile said of the sculpture. "It's something that needed to be done a long time ago. It establishes who we really are. We've been put down for so long. Now, we're up there."

Marshall Coach Bobby Pruett said he was thrilled and honored to participate in the ceremony, even with the kickoff to the biggest game of the season just minutes away.

"This is truly a wonderful piece of work," Pruett said. "It's a wonderful, beautiful, loving idea."

Pruett called Marshall's rise from the ashes of the crash to national prominence "truly God's miracle."

The crowd attending the ceremony filled much of the parking lot. It began gathering in the area of the unveiling early, spurred by the peaceful sounds of MU grad Tom Palmer's bagpipes.

When it ended, many moved in to get a close-up look at the statue mounted on a new brick wall. It was created by artist Burl Jones of Sissonville, W.Va., and cost about $150,000.

Many took pictures and videos while others simply gazed at the piece of work for several minutes after the ceremony.

"It's beautiful," said Edith Frasure, a member of the Herd Sideliners, a booster group for the team. "It will always make people remember."

"It's very appropriate," said her friend, Doris Akers.

The spirit of the ceremony carried into the game as noisy Herd fans packed into the stadium on a cold, clear night.

"I'm excited and thrilled about the opportunity we have tonight as a football team," Pruett told the crowd. "And, I'm excited and thrilled about this sculpture."

Bart Andrews, a member of the bronze committee which raised funds for the project for more than a year, said people from all over the country sent in donations.

"I'm pleased they understand what it's all about," Andrews said.

Marshall President Dan Angel likes the name of the bronze—"We Are Marshall."

"To me it says, 'We are Marshall, still,' " Angel said. "We were then, are now and always will be."

WSAZ-3 sports director Keith Morehouse, whose father, Gene, died in the crash, said he's often reminded to "never take anything for granted."

"When you cheer," he softly asked the crowd, "give a little extra cheer for the team that never made it home."

THE YOUNG HERD

A STORY OF TRIUMPH

September 18, 1971

THE LONG ROAD BACK

MARSHALL BOWS, 29-6: MOREHEAD WINS '71 OPENER

By Mike Brown, The Herald-Advertiser

MOREHEAD, Ky.—Marshall University's Young Thundering Herd started that long trail back Saturday night and the biggest disappointment was the score.

The Young Herd, playing for the first time since last November's air tragedy, acquitted themselves well Saturday night despite dropping a 29-6 decision to Morehead State University's Eagles at Breathitt Sports Center.

A record Morehead crowd of 11,000, an estimated 4,000 of them from Marshall, did not see the rout which many no doubt visualized.

A rugged Marshall defense made the Eagles earn every yard they gained. Morehead led 16-0 at the half and scored its last touchdown with 33 seconds to play.

The Young Thundering Herd, unable to mount the offensive consistency which Coach Jack Lengyel knew it had to have, jolted the Morehead fans and gave Marshall fans hope when it scored with 9:31 left in the third period.

The Young Herd drove 47 yards in seven plays with tight end Tom Smyth scoring the touchdown on a 10-yard pass from quarterback Reggie Oliver.

Oliver hit Smyth on the five and the big 205-pound sophomore literally flattened two Morehead defenders as he crashed into the end zone.

The Herd had gained possession on the 47 when it recovered an Eagle fumble.

After Dave Hamilton picked up one yard, Oliver hit wide receiver Lanny Steed over the middle for 20 years to the 28.

Oliver then lost five yards before hitting Steed again for 17 yards and when Morehead's Harry "Sugar Bear" Lyles was called for a personal foul, the ball was placed on the nine. Hamilton then lost two yards on two consecutive plays before Oliver hit Smyth for the score.

Oliver rolled to the right and just lofted the ball to Smyth who then bulled his way into the end zone.

Morehead had a total offense of 443 yards, 304 on the ground, but the Herd made the Eagles cough up the football four times on fumbles.

Middle guard Odell Graves and linebacker Rick Meckstroth were the defensive leaders for the Herd, each being in on 14 tackles. Graves, a freshman from Erie, Pa., made 12 individual tackles and Meckstroth 10.

Graves also recovered one fumble while Gene Nance covered two and sophomore defensive end Gary Dorsey one.

Marshall head football coach Jack Lengyel, center, poses with Young Thundering Herd players during media day in 1971.

After the Marshall touchdown, the Eagles drove to the Herd 14 where the defense held as the third period ended.

The Eagles made it 23-6 on their first series of the fourth quarter with quarterback Dave Schaetzke scampering around left end from seven yards out for the touchdown. Kirk Andrews then booted the extra point.

The Herd was unable to mount another offensive threat after its score as the Morehead defense tightened.

Coach Jake Hallum began sprinkling his lineup with reserves with about seven minutes remaining and reserve quarterback Lou Mains took Morehead in for its final score.

Frank Jones, who was not listed on the Eagles' three-deep depth chart, scored it on a one-yard run.

Schaetzke, as expected, was the show for the Eagles. The Toledo, Ohio, sophomore picked up 87 yards rushing in 15 attempts and completed 13 of 23 passes for 109 yards.

John Coning added 66 yards rushing on 13 attempts while Marshall's top ground gainer was tailback John Johnstonbaugh with 57 yards on nine carries, all in the first half. Oliver completed seven of 14 passes for 78 yards with Smyth catching three for 33 yards.

Marshall managed one serious scoring threat in the first half when, thanks to a 39-yard scamper by John Johnstonbaugh, it drove to the Morehead seven-yard line.

However, the veteran Eagle defense stiffened and on fourth and goal from the eight, Tom Feely's 25-yard field goal attempt was wide to the left.

Johnstonbaugh's sprint stunned the Eagles who had taken a 9-0 lead on the previous series on Kirk Andrews' 27-yard field goal with 9:39 left in the half.

FOUL HELPS

Dave Hamilton returned the ensuing kickoff 18 yards to the Marshall 24. The Young Herd, aided by a 15-yard personal foul call on Harry Lyles, moved to the Morehead 47 in four plays with Oliver picking up three yards for a first down.

After Terry Gardner picked up one yard to the 46, Johnstonbaugh hit off left tackle and broke to the sideline and needed only one block to have gone all the way.

The Eagles, who did not get their first down of the game until the 5:18 mark in the first period, scored with 13 seconds left in the first half when Cason scored on a 23-yard run over left tackle.

The stocky 5-8, 190-pound Cason, Morehead's leading ground gainer the last two seasons, was hit hard at the 13 but spun and continued into the end zone. It capped a drive which started on the Morehead 29 following a 44-yard punt by Ron Eshbaugh.

NEED SIX PLAYS

It took the Eagles only six plays to score with the big gainer coming when Schaetzke hit split end Mo Hollingsworth for 23 yards. Morehead missed the extra point when the center snap was low.

Andrews' field goal was set up on a 33-yard punt return by Hollingsworth which carried to the Marshall 27.

McCray carried two straight times for a first down at the 15. However, the Herd defense stiffened and on third-and-four, Schaetzke was thrown for a three-yard loss. Andrews, who missed two field goals from close range in MSU's 7-7 tie with Marshall in 1968, booted it through the uprights with 9:39 left in the half.

The Eagles made it 16-0 with 34 seconds left in the half when Schaetzke, surrounded by three Herd defenders, rifled a five-yard pass to John High in the end zone on third down.

The score climaxed an 80-yard drive following Fooly's abortive field goal attempt. The drive required 13 plays with Schaetzke picking up 43 on the ground and passing for another 13.

Marshall head coach Jack Lengyel, right, gives instructions to Young Thundering Herd quarterback Reggie Oliver during the Young Herd's game against Morehead State in 1971.

LENGYEL UNBOWED; HALLUM PLEASED

By Lowell Cade, The Herald-Advertiser

New Marshall head coach Jack Lengyel led the Young Herd in 1971, taking over the task of rebuilding the team. He resigned four years later, saddened by the need to replace the walk-on players of the Young Herd with a scholarship-caliber team to compete against quality opponents.

MOREHEAD—One game doesn't make a season, but this one Saturday night between Marshall University and Morehead State was a big one.

The Young Thundering Herd of Coach Jack Lengyel played its first game—and lost—since the airplane crash last Nov. 14, near Huntington which took the lives of 25 Marshall players and head coach Rick Tolley.

"It's a start," said Lengyel, who came down to Huntington from the College of Wooster to reconstruct the MU football program. "It's a start ... we'll grow each week," he said.

Morehead, a veteran team and the favorite to win the Ohio Valley Conference championship, defeated the Young Herd 29-6. "We worked hard for this game, too," said a pleased Jake Hallum, the Morehead coach.

Lengyel wanted to make one thing clear: "Morehead is not our season," he said. "Ten games is our season. How we stand up to that challenge is our objective for the year."

In spite of the defeat and the many mistakes the sophomore-freshman dominated MU team made, there were glimmers of hope. A young quarterback, Reggie Oliver, directed his team to one touchdown, capping the 53-yard drive with a 10-yard alley-oop pass to tight end Tom Smyth.

Smyth, a 205-pounder from Cincinnati, was pleased that he scored Marshall's first new era touchdown.

"It was my first touchdown as a college varsity player," he smiled, "and the fact that it came in our first game, under these circumstances, makes it that much more enjoyable." He wished, however, there could have been more.

GAINS 57 YARDS

Another sophomore, John Johnstonbaugh, was Marshall's leading ground gainer against a defense that could be one of the roughest, and most experienced the Herd will have to face this season.

Johnstonbaugh gained 57 yards on nine carries, all in the first half, and almost broke loose once for a touchdown, a 39-yard burst from the MSU 46 to the seven.

"It was just one of our basic plays," said Oliver. "We call it 15. That's the way our offense is. One time we get three or four yards, and the next time—boom, you break for a long gainer. We're going to get better. There'll be more long ones like that."

HONEST MISTAKES

Lengyel said his team made a lot of mistakes, but was quick to point out that they were "honest mistakes, not mistakes out of a lack of effort."

Hallum was quick to point out in defense of the MU defeat, "those kids came out for the second half and went right to score (the first time the Herd had the ball in the third quarter). They were hitting all the way! With that kind of attitude, they're going to give some people a bad time one of these days."

DEFENSE CRACKING

Lengyel complimented his defense. "It got us the ball several times," he said. "And it was cracking. That football got jarred loose a few times (from MSU backs) out there."

However, he was also aware that Marshall's punt and kickoff coverage wasn't as good as it can be. "We tended to cave in toward the ball instead of staying in our lanes.

"Morehead is strong. Their backs run with authority, and because of it they got five yards when maybe they should only have gotten three, and three when they shouldn't have gotten any.

"And (Dave) Schaetzke ... he's just a good running quarterback." The MSU sophomore ran for 87 yards and passed for 109.

Hallum was concerned about his team's offensive turnovers. The Eagles lost four fumbles—two in each half, and two inside the Marshall 20-yard line.

"That plagued us all last year," said Hallum. "Now we're pleased."

YOUNG HERD DOES IT

MU 15, XAVIER 13: SCORES TOUCHDOWN ON FINAL PLAY

By Lowell Cade, The Herald-Advertiser

Marshall University's Young Thundering Herd stunned Xavier, 15-13, here Saturday and it's doubtful any Marshall team ever won a bigger game or a more dramatic one.

The victory at Fairfield Stadium before an estimated record crowd of 13,000, including Gov. Arch A. Moore Jr., came just ten months and 11 days after the jetliner crash of Nov. 14, 1970, that dealt football at MU a staggering blow.

A record crowd of 13,000 fans, including West Virginia Governor Arch Moore, witnesses Marshall's stunning upset of Xavier University, September 25, 1971. It was the team's first victory in the post-crash era.

And so it is—time has not run out on Marshall football. And it did not run out Saturday. The winning touchdown came on the last play of the game, and it signaled just the beginning for the Young Herd.

Fleet Terry Gardner, a freshman fullback from Portsmouth, Ohio, took a screen pass for 13 yards and the score. Reggie Oliver, a sophomore quarterback from Tuscaloosa, Ala., threw it. The play is titled "213 bootleg screen." And it's one that Marshall fans will remember for a long, long time.

When the Herd lined up there were eight seconds on the scoreboard clock and by the time MU tackle Jack Crabtree cut down Xavier's Leo Burby the game was over. Burby, a defensive tackle, was the only man with a shot at the sprinting Gardner, and Crabtree, a sophomore from Tazewell, Va., laid him low.

Pandemonium erupted—both on the AstroTurfed field and in the refurbished Fairfield stands. There was no reason to try to restore order and attempt the extra point.

Oliver did not look the part of the neophyte making only his second varsity start as he directed his team 48 yards in 10 plays for the winning score. Including the winning toss, the 6-2, 190-pounder completed five of ten throws in a minute and 18 seconds. That's all the time that was left after George Jackson fielded John Phillips'

punt at the Xavier 49 and returned it one yard.

Oliver dug himself a hole, though, missing three passes from the 48 before hitting Jerry Arrasmith for 11 yards and a first down at the 37. Then Reggie came right back with a sideline pattern to Kelly Sherwood for a carbon copy pickup to the 26.

The air game almost backfired on the next play, an attempt to tight end Tom Smyth, as the Musketeers' Stan Thompson had an interception in his hands but let it slip away.

Oliver wasn't through with Smyth, though, clicking for an eight-yard gain before having an attempt to Arrasmith batted away by Musky linebacker Dick West. The clock stopped with 20 seconds showing.

On fourth and two, Oliver picked on Arrasmith again, this time over the middle for five yards and a first down at the 13. That set up the scoring pass to Gardner.

The winning play was inserted into the MU play book just this week. "Two-13 bootleg" was one of the few passes that went well last Saturday when Marshall opened with a 29-6 loss at Morehead. On the suggestion of receiver coach Red Dawson, a screen off similar play action was designed.

Young Herd quarterback Reggie Oliver set team career records for passing attempts (560) and completions (240), and will always be remembered for the victory over Xavier. Later that year, Marshall would upset highly touted Bowling Green, coached by Don Nehlen, who later became the long-time coach of West Virginia University. Bowling Green had been expected to go to the Peach Bowl before losing to Marshall.

With one second in the game, quarterback Reggie Oliver hit tailback Terry Gardner on a bootleg pass and Gardner scampered 13 yards for the winning touchdown as the Young Herd defeated Xavier, 15-13.

Oliver tied two records with the touchdown strike to Gardner, setting his passing totals for the day at 20-for-43. The 20 completions matched a record set at Oxford, Ohio, in 1969 by Bobby Harris against Miami. And his 43 attempts equaled Ted Shoebridge's total of last September at Toledo.

For the day the air game of Oliver and David Walsh, who hit one of four for 16 yards, totaled 256 yards, and Oliver alone passed for 240.

The latter ranks third by an individual behind Shoebridge's 312 against Ohio U in 1969 and Howard Lee Miller's 234 against Buffalo in 1964.

The Herd's 21 first downs—15 passing and three each by the rush and penalties—were only four short of school standard.

Freshman split end Lanny Steed was the favorite target pulling in eight aerials for 113 yards.

Sharing Marshall scoring with Gardner were Blakely Smith and Oliver. Smith, a walk-on soccer-style place kicker, playing in his first football game ever, put the Young Herd on the scoreboard in the first quarter with a 31-yard field goal. Oliver capped a 73-yard fourth-quarter march with a two-yard quarterback keeper that put MU on top 9-6 with 11:58 remaining in the game.

Xavier, which went down to its second defeat of the season, got a touchdown in the third quarter on a one-yard plunge by Ivy Williams, and on a 48-yard punt return by John Gompers in the last period.

Gompers' starting run came with just 4:09 left in the final stanza, and Ed Huber's placement gave the Musketeers a 13-9 margin.

Defensively the Herd stopped the Musketeers inside its 20 yard line twice—once at the 12 before the end of the first half, and at the 13 just before Gompers' scoring punt return.

The Musketeers were also stopped at the Herd 33, 37 and 27, falling twice on fourth down and short yardage situations. Leading tacklers for Marshall were linebackers Charles Henry and Rick Meckstroth, in on 20 and 18, respectively, and middle guard O'dell Graves with 17. Graves was high in solos with three, while Henry had two.

Chuck Wright and Graves led in tackles for losses, costing the Musketeers 26 and 14 yards.

The game began as a punting duel. John Phillips of X, who booted ten times and averaged 44.5 per try, was matched on occasions by MU's freshman Bob Eshbaugh.

Marshall got its first scoring drive untracked last in the first quarter from the Xavier 32 after stopping the Muskies on a fourth-and-two. Helped along by a pass interference call for a first down at the X 47, Oliver marched his team 54 yards to the Xavier 14 nine plays. Key plays were passes of 18 yards to fullback Randy Kerr, and 12 to Steed.

On fourth-and-seven, Blakely Smith came on to test his soccer-style kick and as the first quarter ended put three points on the board.

The Herd didn't threaten in the second quarter, but the Green defense stopped Xavier at its 37 and 12.

MARCO DELAYS PLAY

The second half was delayed approximately five minutes as members of The Robe, an MU leadership organization, and spectators corralled a loose and irritated Marco, Marshall's mascot buffalo.

After three plays, the Herd was forced to punt. Eshbaugh's boot rolled dead at the MU 49, but an Xavier clip moved the ball back to the Xavier 36. From there the Musketeers showed the power offense they are noted for as Al Banks and Ivy Williams slashed the MU defense for 48 yards, and quarterback Paul Smith hit two of four passes for 25 more.

Fans celebrate the "miracle" victory by the Young Herd over Xavier University September 25, 1971. On the same day, Wichita State celebrated its first post-crash victory. Lengyel credited assistant coach Red Dawson, a member of the 1970 staff who did not fly home with the team from East Carolina, for calling the play that won the game.

Banks got a key run on the drive, picking up 26 yards on third-and-27 from the X 42 of the MU 31. Williams got the first down. Smith scrambled for 11 yards and a first down on third-and-seven, then flipped 12 yards to Williams for a first down at the one. Williams plunged in for the score.

SECOND ATTEMPT WIDE

Huber, a lefty kicker, converted but Xavier was penalized for illegal procedure, and his second attempt was wide. Xavier had a 6-3 lead, and carried it into the final quarter.

Three plays into the last period, the Herd stopped an Xavier thrust at 27 when Gary Dorsey, a defensive end, broke up Tim Dydo's fourth-and-two pass intended for Banks.

Oliver started the Herd toward its first touchdown with an option play on which he lateraled to John Johnstonbaugh for 12 yards. Then he went to the air. He hit Steed for 14, Sherwood for nine, Steed again for seven and the Herd was on the Xavier 31.

Oliver's next pass, intended for Gardner, was incomplete, but a personal foul against Xavier gave MU a first down at the 16. Oliver went right back to Gardner and the speedster from Portsmouth West high just missed by two yards scoring both touchdowns. Reggie carried in on the next play with 11:58 remaining to play. Blakely Smith's try for the point after failed, but Marshall was back on top, 9-6.

After the Herd forced a Musky punt, the losers appeared to get a break when they recovered a Gardner fumble at the Marshall 41. Smith moved his team to the Marshall 13, but turned over the football when he tried to run out of the pocket on fourth-and-four only to run into Gene Nance one yard short.

Terry Gardner, left, and Reggie Oliver celebrate after the Young Thundering Herd's 15-13 victory over Xavier in 1971. Gardner caught a screen pass from Oliver and raced to the end zone for the winning score on the final play of the game.

From its ten, Marshall couldn't move and Eshbaugh pointed to Gompers at the MU 48. Gompers started up the middle, was hit, and spun to the east sideline which was wide open. The score at 4:09 painted a bleak picture for Coach Lengyel's crew.

Inside the two-minute mark, and Xavier on its own 25, Chuck Wright nailed Smith for a nine-yard loss on third-and-four. That turned the ball over to the Herd for its last bow.

And what a bow!

Next Saturday Marshall will take its 1-1 record against Miami in Oxford. Saturday, the Redskins played a night contest in Dayton.

MU COOL LIKE LENGYEL

By Mike Brown, The Herald-Advertiser

A football team nearly always reflects the personality of the head coach.

Marshall University's victorious Young Thundering Herd did just that Saturday afternoon when it shocked Xavier University, 15-13, for a victory which many felt would be much longer coming.

"They held their poise and stayed in there," said Coach Jack Lengyel in the celebrating Marshall dressing room minutes after Terry Gardner had scored his dramatic touchdown.

While those around him were hardly able to contain themselves, Lengyel calmly stood in his Fairfield Stadium office wiping his forehead with a towel.

How, someone asked Lengyel, can you stay so calm at such a moment?

"I usually don't get excited," he grinned. "I just get a little upset sometimes when things don't go right."

Lengyel had very little to get upset about Saturday as his Young Herd stunned the Musketeers and the estimated record crowd of 13,000 who were on hand to see Marshall win in only its second game of the season.

"It was a total team effort—a 60-minute total team effort," he said. "That's the only way you could describe it."

STORY BOOK FINISH

"It was a storybook finish," he added. "No one thought we had a chance to win except the team."

Marshall, which nursed first a 3-0 and then a 9-6 lead, saw its hopes of victory apparently go down the drain when John Gompers, a product of Wheeling Central High School, scoot 48 yards with a punt to give Xavier a 13-9 lead with 4:09 to play.

"We told them to keep their heads up," said Lengyel, "that they still had four minutes to do something with the ball."

Marshall then got the football back for one last crack with 1:18 left on the Xavier 48.

DEFENSE OUTSTANDING

"The defense did an outstanding job all day," pointed out Lengyel. "When the offense started moving the ball in the second half, it took a lot of pressure off of them."

The Herd offense, directed by quarterback Reggie Oliver, coolly moved in for the score. Twice Oliver passed for the first down on fourth down, once hitting Jerry Arrasmith for 11 yards on fourth-and-10 and again to Arrasmith for eight on fourth-and-two.

Then came the clinching heave to Gardner who scored when Jack Crabtree flattened Xavier's Leo Burby.

"That's the greatest block I'ver ever seen," said Gardner, a freshman from Portsmouth. "I couldn't believe Jack got out there as quickly as he did. He was the only guy that had a shot at me and when I saw the block, I knew I had a touchdown."

LAST-MINUTE STARTER

Oliver was a last-minute starter and nearly didn't get back in for the final scoring drive when he suffered a bump on the elbow midway through the fourth period.

"The team doctor told us Reggie could go back in," said Lengyel who decided to start Oliver over Dave Walsh when he watched both of them warm up in pre-game drills.

RED CALLED WINNER

"I was watching them (Oliver and Walsh) warm up and it was then that I decided to start Reggie," Lengyel explained.

"He has poise, is a team leader and throws well," he added, "and I knew we had to throw the ball to beat Xavier."

"Red (Dawson) made the call on the winning play," said offensive coordinator Jim McNally. "We talked about it over the phone, but it was Red's call."

The Marshall defense had a field day, too, and defensive coordinator John Riley pointed out, "We didn't have a substitution all day—those eleven guys went all the way."

Defensive line coach Andy Nameth, who was an assistant coach at Ohio State for two years, ushered a big grin and said, "This was greater than the Rose Bowl win the year we beat O.J. (Simpson) and Southern Cal.

"The defensive line simply did a great job."

MU COACH LOOKS TO THE FUTURE

LENGYEL: WE'LL BE BETTER

By Lowell Cade, The Herald-Advertiser

"We WILL be better . . ."

Jack Lengyel closed out the first season as Marshall University football coach—the greatest challenge ever in collegiate athletics—looking to the future.

His Young Thundering Herd had just absorbed its eighth defeat, 30-0, to arch rival Ohio University at rain-swept Fairfield Stadium. But, the Herd won two more games than most expected, the wins coming over Xavier in the home opener, and over Bowling Green to delight a homecoming throng.

Bill Rohr, athletic director of Ohio, interrupted Lengyel's discussion with newsmen just long enough to set the tone.

"Your freshmen have come a long way," said Rohr. "They gave our varsity a helluva football game."

Marshall ran into trouble in the second quarter, two fumbles setting up two Ohio touchdowns.

MISTAKES HAVE HURT

"Mistakes have plagued us all year," mused Lengyel, at the same time trying to rationalize. "But, we're a young football team, we can't lose sight of that, and we just haven't been consistent on offense."

Lengyel shouldered some of the blame for his team's troubles in the second quarter, drawing a 15-yard penalty for "unsportsmanlike conduct," going onto the field protesting OU's first touchdown.

The play was a six-yard pass from Dave Juenger to Tim Worner. Worner took the pass going out of the end zone on the west sideline.

"He had a foot in bounds when the pass first hit his hand," said Lengyel, "but I protested whether he had possession until after he was off the field. I still question it. But the penalty was my fault. I shouldn't have gone onto the field."

CAUGHT FLAT-FOOTED

The 15 yards were stepped off against the Herd on the OU kickoff. The Bobcats caught the irritated Herd flat-footed with an onside boot, kicker Dave Green covering at the MU 34.

OU didn't convert the good field position into a score. Green's 27-yard field goal attempt missing. But, on the next MU play from the 20, freshman quarterback Steve Cooper was cut down by Jack LeVeck and his fumble opened the scoring door for the Bobcats again.

Lengyel started with an all-freshman backfield, as he'd indicated before the game. Cooper was directing from quarterback while Ned Burks and Terry Gardner were the runners.

OLIVER COMES ON

Cooper gave way to sophomore Reggie Oliver mid-way through the second quarter, and after Cooper had been tackled hard, fumbling at his 19 to set up an easy OU touchdown.

"We rotated our quarterbacks," Lengyel continued, "trying to ignite a spark (under the offense). Burks is running well, but after the second quarter we know we've got to throw the football if we're going to catch up."

Cooper and Oliver combined hit 10 of 21 passes, but weren't connecting long. Their completions were limited to flairs, look-ins and screens for just 63 yards.

44-YARD GALLOP

Burks gained 79 yards on 10 carries, and had Marshall's longest run from scrimmage, 44 yards from his own 45 to the OU 11. The Bobcat defense, however, rose up and stalled the Herd's best scoring bid.

Looking at the entire season, Lengyel is "proud of the effort. I think the kids have done a fine job, and as I said before I'm sure we'll get better.

"We've got a good nucleus to build around. The team's got to stay together. It did the best it could this year. It's been a good year in that respect; and that's all we, as coaches, can expect."

The game was the last for senior defensive back Nate Ruffin, who was forced to leave the game early in the third quarter with a hand injury.

"I got it tangled in someone's helmet," said the Marshall captain, forcing a smile and recalling he "got a few good licks in before I had to come out."

He wanted so much to close out with a victory, but it just wasn't to be. Ruffin is one of three surviving varsity players from last year's team, missing the ill-fated flying trip to East Carolina last November because of an arm injury that has hampered his play all season. The others are juniors Flip Jordan and Ed Carter.

Ruffin's plans are incomplete, but there could be a spot for him on Lengyel's staff as a graduate assistant next fall.

"I guess this was my last game of organized football," he said.

EMOTIONS OF TRAGEDY DREW
LENGYEL TO MARSHALL

By David Walsh, The Herald-Dispatch

HUNTINGTON—Coach Jack Lengyel had returned home from a successful day at the office. Lengyel, head football coach at the College of Wooster in 1970, directed the Fighting Scots to a 9-6 win at Oberlin College on the afternoon of Nov. 14. At home that evening with his wife, Sandy, they saw a bulletin on TV about the plane bringing the Marshall football team back from its game at East Carolina crashing.

"My heart just sank," said Lengyel during a Huntington visit. "The atmosphere of players, coaches and fans. It's like it's your team."

Lengyel and Thundering Herd backers in the Tri-State and across West Virginia finally got the news no one wanted to hear. There were no survivors in the traveling party of 75 people.

"You pray someone survives," Lengyel said. "But it's hope against hope. I thought, 'Oh my God!' There's that fraternity of athletics, that bond. I imagine every coach in the country had that same hollow feeling."

Marshall head coach Rick Tolley was among the crash victims.

Lengyel was named to take Tolley's place on March 12, 1971. He accepted the job after the first choice, Dick Bestwick, backed out after staying for a week and returned to Georgia Tech.

"I believe I called them," Lengyel said. "They've got to find somebody. It never bothered me about Dick leaving. They needed leadership."

Lengyel, who went from walk-on to scholarship player at the University of Akron, found himself in an NCAA Division I environment with limited resources. His 1971 team was made up of returning players who didn't make the East Carolina trip, members of the 1970 freshman team and walk-ons.

"I had a chance to give back to football what football gave to me," he said. "I wanted to be a part of this. I wanted to help rebuild. It was an overwhelming challenge, but one I thought we could accomplish."

After his arrival, Lengyel found the damage went deeper. "It was more than football recovering. It was a town recovering," he said.

The Young Thundering Herd, as Lengyel called the team until a four-year class structure was established, won two games in 1971 (Xavier and Bowling Green). After four years and a 9-33 overall record, Lengyel left Marshall and went into business. He later got into athletic administration and served as athletic director at Louisville, Missouri, Fresno State and the Naval Academy where he retired in 2001.

Starting in 1984, the Herd started fielding winning teams. Marshall went on to dominate the Southern Conference and Mid-American Conference, won league and national titles, had Heisman Trophy candidates and moved into a 38,000-seat stadium. This is year one for Marshall in Conference USA. The city has made a rebound, too, with things such as the opening of Pullman Square.

It's quite a turnaround from 1971 and that's what makes Nov. 14 memorable for Lengyel wherever he is.

"When the curtain's pulled back, you relive the moments," Lengyel said. "You see faces, people and remember the events. It was bigger than the football team. It was about the struggle of a community.

"You see Pullman Square and what the football team's done, it's all about progress. It (Nov. 14) is always special."

Former Marshall head football coach Jack Lengyel poses for a scene of the "We Are Marshall" movie on Marshall's campus on Tuesday, April 11, 2006. The movie tells of the 1970 plane crash that killed 75 people including members of the football team and the fight to keep the football program. Lengyel coached the team following the crash.

THE YOUNG HERD

NATE RUFFIN BECAME VICTIMS' VOICE

The Herald-Dispatch

Nate Ruffin was a last-minute scratch from the Marshall football team chartered jet to the Nov. 14, 1970, game at East Carolina.

Ruffin was an injured defensive back, but still anticipated making the trip. At the last minute, he and a few other injured players were told that school boosters would take their seats on the jet, The Associated Press reported. On the flight back from Greenville, N.C., the jet crashed short of Tri-State Airport and all 75 people aboard died—including most of the football team.

Left behind on campus, Ruffin passed the time by going downtown to a movie theater. That's where he heard the terrible news.

The Associated Press reported that Ruffin never knew—and didn't care to find out—who took his seat on the charter.

Ruffin became the team spokesman and leader after the tragedy. He helped take phone calls from parents and was asked to assist in identifying bodies. He helped bring the players together in 1971 as the team captain when the football program resumed.

At the 1997 induction ceremony of the Black Legends of Marshall—where Ruffin represented his fallen teammates—he said today's athletes probably don't know all they should about how the crash affected the campus and the community.

During the ceremony Ruffin talked about a Sports Illustrated article where Marshall star Randy Moss was quoted as saying the plane crash "was a tragedy, but it really wasn't nothing big."

Ruffin said he met privately with Moss after the article came out.

"The ground you're walking on was paved by many black men and many white

Sophomore defensive back Felix Jordan (left) and junior defensive back Nate Ruffin (center) missed the trip to East Carolina, along with a handful of other players, because of injuries. Ruffin would return to Marshall often through the years to witness Marshall's rise to national prominence.

Marshall 1971 senior captain Nate Ruffin, left, and head coach Jack Lengyel.

Former Marshall football co-captain of the 1970 team Nate Ruffin, right, listens along with current head football coach Bobby Pruett during the 30th anniversary service Nov. 14, 2000, for the 75 people killed in the Marshall plane crash.

men," Ruffin said he told Moss. "I was left behind so I could tell the story for those men who are not around now. As long as I live, I shall tell the story. As long as we tell the story, they shall live."

Ruffin is being played by Anthony Mackie in the "We Are Marshall" movie.

Ruffin died in October 2001 at age 51 from leukemia.

At the time of his death he was vice president of community relations with The Freedom Forum, an Arlington, Va.-based foundation "dedicated to free press, free speech and free spirit for all people," according to its Web site.

He also put in time as personnel manager at ACF Industries in Huntington and worked as the human resources director for The Herald-Dispatch.

Ruffin is buried at Spring Hill Cemetery next to six players who died in the crash whose bodies could not be identified and former Marshall assistant athletic director Ed Starling.

He is survived by his wife, Sharon, and three children, Carmen, Shante and Ryan.

THE YOUNG HERD

RED DAWSON HELPED MOLD 1971 TEAM

The Herald-Dispatch

Red Dawson was somewhere around Greensboro, N.C., when he heard the news.

The Marshall football team he had helped coach only hours earlier had been involved in a plane crash. Later, he learned that all 75 people aboard the DC-9 jet carrying the team, staff and some supporters back from Greenville, N.C., to Huntington died in the crash near Tri-State Airport.

Marshall lost its game that day to East Carolina. Rather than flying back with the team on that foggy, rainy Nov. 14, 1970, night, Dawson, who had been on the road recruiting, drove back.

On the drive home, he learned about the plane crash by radio.

The 27-year-old Dawson helped hold the football program together following the tragedy. He remained on the Marshall coaching staff one more year and was instrumental in helping new head coach Jack Lengyel rebuild the Young Thundering Herd.

Today, the 60-something Valdosta, Ga., native operates a Huntington construction company.

He has also been closely involved with the making of "We Are Marshall," the Warner Bros. movie that chronicles the story of the plane crash and rebirth of the football program. Actor Matthew Fox is playing Dawson in the movie, with dyed red hair to match.

Dawson was a star end at Florida State, where he is a member of the athletic Hall of Fame. He played one year of pro football.

Marshall 1971 receivers coach Red Dawson.

Former Marshall football assistant coach Red Dawson poses in front of the Memorial Fountain at Marshall University on Wednesday, Feb. 1, 2006, in Huntington. Dawson was the Thundering Herd's defensive coordinator when a plane carrying 75 people including fellow coaches and players crashed November 1970 near Huntington Tri-State Airport. Dawson was not on the plane back from East Carolina because he was making a recruiting trip. The following year Dawson stayed with the team as a receivers coach.

Actor Matthew Fox, left, laughs with former Marshall assistant coach Red Dawson during a break in the filming of "We Are Marshall" on Tuesday, April 4, 2006, near Twin Towers on Marshall's campus in Huntington, W.Va. Fox is portraying Dawdson in the movie depicting the events surrounding the 1970 plane crash that claimed 75 lives including members of Marshall's football team.